AMERICA'S ROAD TO SOCIALISM

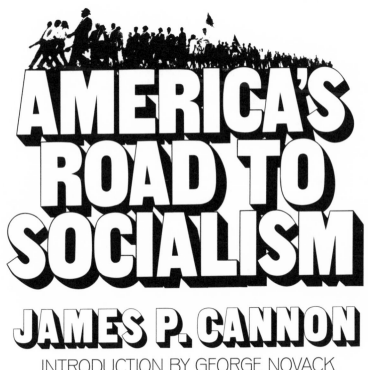

AMERICA'S ROAD TO SOCIALISM

JAMES P. CANNON

INTRODUCTION BY GEORGE NOVACK

PATHFINDER

New York   London   Montreal   Sydney

America's Road to Socialism was first presented as a six-part series of public forums in Los Angeles, California, in December 1952 and January 1953. The last five parts of the series, included in this edition, were first published in the socialist newsweekly *The Militant* on January 12, January 26, February 16, March 23, March 30, and July 26, 1953. The entire series was published by Pioneer Publishers in October 1953.

Copyright © 1975 by Pathfinder Press
All rights reserved

ISBN 0-87348-417-7 paper; ISBN 0-87348-416-9 cloth
Library of Congress Catalog Card Number 74-26234
Manufactured in the United States of America

First (Pioneer) edition, 1953
Second edition, 1975
Third printing, 2002

Pathfinder

410 West Street, New York, NY 10014, U.S.A.
Fax: (212) 727-0150
E-mail: pathfinderpress@compuserve.com

PATHFINDER DISTRIBUTORS AROUND THE WORLD:
Australia (and Asia and the Pacific):
    Pathfinder, Level 1, 3/281-287 Beamish St., Campsie, NSW 2194
    Postal address: P.O. Box K879, Haymarket, NSW 1240
Canada:
    Pathfinder, 2761 Dundas St. West, Toronto, ON, M6P 1Y4
Iceland:
    Pathfinder, Klapparstíg 26, 2d floor, 101 Reykjavík
    Postal address: P. Box 0233, IS 121 Reykjavík
New Zealand:
    Pathfinder, P.O. Box 3025, Auckland
Sweden:
    Pathfinder, Domargränd 16, S-129 47, Hägersten
United Kingdom (and Europe, Africa except South Africa, and Middle East):
    Pathfinder, 47 The Cut, London, SE1 8LL
United States (and Caribbean, Latin America, and South Africa):
    Pathfinder, 410 West Street, New York, NY 10014

CONTENTS

OTHER BOOKS BY JAMES P. CANNON

INTRODUCTION

Supporters of the established order have little doubt about what the future holds for the American people. As the Gershwin lyric goes: "Castles may tumble, Gibraltar may crumble, they're only made of clay, but" capitalism is here to stay—indefinitely.

U.S. capitalism is so rich, so productive, so almighty, so deeply rooted "in the hearts of our countrymen," that it can never be dislodged and replaced, they fervently believe. Because of its inherent strength, its special path of development precludes the possibility of revolutionary changes. These may occur elsewhere, but they are foreign to America.

From this perspective, socialism has no future on American soil. A revolution based upon an upheaval of the working masses is a pipe dream. Most wage workers are so snugly incorporated into the "consumer society" of the corporate hucksters that they will never aspire to seek anything better or to go beyond it. "America's Road to Socialism" is a utopian fantasy without relevance to the realities of our national life or our political future.

In this book James P. Cannon controverts such conventional wisdom, shared by liberals and conservatives alike. He holds to the contrary that socialism is the only progressive alternative to monopolist and militarist misrule, that it is both a liberating and realistic goal, and that it must be foreseen and prepared, organized and fought for. He peers beyond the coming struggle for power between the rulers and the ruled. Predicting a victory for the workers and their allies, he asks: What could this country become under the leadership of a different class, one that is motivated not by the pursuit of profit at all costs but by concern for the welfare and culture of the working people who create the wealth?

Many individuals, disgusted with the intolerable evils of American capitalism, have exclaimed at one time or another: "There must be a better way of living and making a living than this one!" There is, there can be. That is the essential message presented and argued in these pages. A socialist America, operating with a planned economy under democratic control of the working people, could assure everyone the basic necessities of food, clothing, and housing and provide an increasing abundance of material benefits and cultural advantages that would radically transform the habits, customs, and relations of human beings for the better. Such a system would eventually eradicate oppressive inequalities of all kinds and enhance individual opportunities and freedoms in a fraternal atmosphere of social solidarity.

This vision of what a socialist future could achieve in contrast to the capitalist way of life is the most inspiring feature of this work. It can act as an antidote to the widespread apprehension that a successful socialist revolution in this country might have the same result as the worker-peasant revolutions in the first half of this century, which have led to the establishment of bureaucratic dictatorships. Nothing has done more to discredit the appeal of socialism than the "monstrosity of Stalinism." Cannon points out the specific historical factors responsible for the bureaucratization of the post-capitalist states and explains why they will not be repeated when the workers come to power in the United States. The American socialist revolution will unfold under diametrically different circumstances and will thereby be able to avoid the difficulties and deformations that have beset the pioneer revolutions in the more backward countries.

James P. Cannon, who died on August 21, 1974, at the age of eighty-four, was one of the eminent veterans of the revolutionary movement both internationally and in the United States. For almost seven decades he devoted his energies to the socialist cause and was involved in the building of a revolutionary party that can guide the workers and their allies to victory on a national and international scale.

He began his career as a volunteer organizer for the Industrial Workers of the World and became a member of the Socialist Party's internationalist and antiwar left wing during the First World War. Inspired by the Russian Revolution, he became a prominent founder of the Communist Party, the first editor of its daily paper, *The Toiler*, later renamed *The Worker*, and a delegate to congresses of the Third International in the 1920s. After his expulsion from the Communist Party in 1928 for his fidelity to Leninism and opposition to Stalinism, he became the prime organizer and leader of the Trotskyist movement in the United States, a founder of the International Left Opposition, and, as a close collaborator of Leon Trotsky, a founder of the Fourth International in 1938. At the time of his death, he was National Chairman Emeritus of the Socialist Workers Party.

Cannon carried forward the heroic traditions of such working-class figures as "Big Bill" Haywood, Eugene V. Debs, and other pioneer American socialists by blending those traditions with the lessons learned from the Bolsheviks under Lenin and Trotsky. The wealth of knowledge about the ideas and ideals of socialism he gleaned from this exceptional range of experience formed the background and basis for his reflections on capitalism and socialism.

These talks were originally given in December 1952 and January 1953 as a series of weekly forums in Los Angeles. That was at the beginning of the Eisenhower administration. Twenty-two years ago American politics presented a different scene than today. The Korean War, the predecessor of Vietnam, was still raging, but there was no mass resistance to it. Reaction held the country in an iron grip. The anticommunist cold war was a bipartisan policy pursued in the international field. At home McCarthyism was rampant. Liberalism was cowed into acquiescence. Organized labor was dormant and deeply conservatized.

The broad radicalism that had flowered in the 1930s was in total retreat. Leftists of any shade were being persecuted, victimized, jailed. All groups without exception suffered splits, desertions, and attrition.

The prolonged prosperity further strengthened the belief in the perpetual reign of capitalism. Tens of thousands of ex-radicals renounced their former hopes in socialism and concluded a separate peace with the status quo, seeking some safe corner in which to cultivate their private lives. They discarded the last shreds of confidence in the prospects of American socialism. This eclipse of revolutionism, when conformism was the supreme commandment of the day, was a severe test for all partisans of Marxism.

Very few voices were raised at that time in defense of a socialist future for America. Cannon's was one of the most vigorous and forthright. As a leader of the Socialist Workers Party, he affirmed his convictions about the principles of revolutionary Marxism and the necessity for continued intransigent struggle against big business rule. He pointed to the vulnerability of the capitalist colossus at the height of its supremacy when it appeared to be the unchallenged and invincible master of all it surveyed. He declared that for all their power and wealth, the U.S. monopolists were running against the tide of historical progress in the contemporary world and would find that their imperialist sovereignty would not prevail unchallenged for as long as that of their British predecessors in the nineteenth century.

Twenty years later, after Vietnam, the Black ghetto rebellions, the Watergate horrors and Nixon's resignation, and a growing world economic and financial crisis, these perceptions are obvious to millions of Americans. But they were bold predictions to make at the height of the cold-war hysteria when it appeared as though the Washington juggernaut, bristling with nuclear weapons, could easily roll over any and all opposition abroad and at home.

Cannon's fundamental position and outlook has withstood the test of two decades. However, from that vantage point in time, he could not possibly foresee in detail what twists and turns further social struggles and political developments in the country would go through and, above all, what particular pattern a resurgence of radicalism would assume.

When the situation did shift during the 1960s, it displayed certain novel and unexpected features that neither he nor others anticipated. Cannon predicted that the new radicalization would result from an economic downturn and renewed attacks on workers' living standards. From this he construed the dynamic of the coming radicalization much in terms of its predecessor of the 1930s. In that decade the aroused industrial workers, organized into the CIO, took the lead in the procession and pulled other sectors of the discontented along with them.

In fact, the new radicalization developed initially along other lines. The postwar prosperity, which kept labor quiescent, lasted far longer than Cannon anticipated. Indeed, the white workers have still to move forcefully and in large numbers. Instead, other social forces arrayed against the status quo entered into action first and the new radicalization arose in the midst of the longest peacetime capitalist boom in history as the result of the impact of the Black liberation struggle and U.S. intervention in Vietnam.

This time the initiative has been taken by the largest oppressed nationality, the Blacks, who have set the pace in action for others to follow. Cannon recognized then that "the Negroes will play a great and decisive role in the revolution, in alliance with the trade unions and the revolutionary party; and in that grand alliance they will demonstrate and conquer their right to full equality."

Even so, he did not properly assess the progressive character and revolutionary implications of Black nationalism as a power in its own right, expressing the aspirations and aims of the most oppressed and super-exploited body of American workers. Black resistance to racial discrimination and indignities would have a tremendous effect in stimulating and intensifying the anti-capitalist struggle in this country.

This underestimation was not a personal fault; it was shared by the whole radical movement. Moreover, Black nationalism itself did not become a powerful current until the early sixties and the advent of Malcolm X, when it became easier to grasp its significance for both the Black liberation and socialist movements. Cannon himself made a valuable contribution to the reorientation of the American Trotskyists on this question in an article he wrote in 1959 entitled "The Russian Revolution and the American Negro Movement" which is reprinted in his book *The First Ten Years of American Communism*.

This essay traces the history of the attempts of the American radical movement to analyze the role of the Black liberation struggle from the days of the early socialist movement, which saw no independent role for the Black liberation movement, maintaining that racial oppression would be eliminated as a matter of course *after* the revolution; to the attempts of the Soviet leadership to educate the young Communist movement of the early twenties on the importance of Black nationalism as a driving force in the revolution; to the distorted attempts of the Stalinized Communist Party to apply these lessons during the thirties. Cannon concluded that the Black struggle in the U.S., while an integral part of the struggle of the working class as a whole, has an independent dynamic and will play a special role in the coming American revolution. He wrote: "The movement of the Negro people and the movement of militant labor, united and coordinated by a revolutionary party, will solve the Negro problem in the only way it can be solved—by a social revolution."

The role of students is another novel aspect of the new radicalization. Although students had played a role in the thirties radicalization, no one foresaw how important they would become. The "silent generation" of the fifties was followed by the militant student activists of the sixties and seventies, who provided the leadership and the shock troops for the international mass movement against U.S. aggression in Vietnam and continue to play an important role in emerging social struggles.

One of the most strikingly contemporary aspects of Cannon's vision for the future is his remarks on women's liberation. Although he did not foresee the precise tempo of the second wave of feminism that we know today, he did predict a resurgence of the women's movement in the period of socialist reconstruction.

"One thing I'm absolutely sure is going to happen early in the period of the workers' government. . . . there will be a tremendous popular movement of women to bust up this medieval institution of forty million separate kitchens and forty million different housewives cooking, cleaning, scrubbing, and fighting dust. . . . The mass emergence of the socialist women from the confining walls of their individual kitchens will be the greatest jail break in history—and the most beneficent. . . ."

Although Cannon could not predict the details of the third American radicalization of the twentieth century, he did keep the spotlight fixed upon the central role of the working class as the irreplaceable agency destined to confront and combat the capitalists and blaze the trail to workers' power and socialism. Sooner or later, he affirmed, the slumbering giant of American labor will shake off its lethargy and go forward to fulfill its historical mission. On this perspective hangs the future of humanity.

This view of the problems and prospects of American socialism as seen from the early 1950s has already given a generation of radicals a clearer picture of what socialism stands for and promises. It is reprinted here according to the text published in pamphlet form by Pioneer Publishers in October 1953, omitting the first lecture, which was devoted to an analysis of the Eisenhower election victory in 1952. Its republication should induce many new readers to accept Cannon's invitation to join "the great work of preparation for the great tomorrow."

George Novack
November 1974

America's road
to socialism

James P. Cannon addressing New York meeting to protest Smith-Connally antilabor law, 1948.

The international prospects of capitalism and socialism

Almost as soon as I was old enough to look around and see and think for myself, I rebelled against the poverty, injustice, and all-around crookedness of capitalism. I became a socialist and joined the movement when I was a boy, and have been working at it ever since.

And if I made a mistake, I can't say I wasn't warned. Quite a few practical people who were interested in my welfare and thought I was marked for success in life began to shake their heads sadly when they heard me popping off on the street corners about socialism.

"It's a fine idea, son, but it'll never work," I was told. "It's against human nature." "There always have been rich and poor and there always will be. Be a realist. Don't waste your life on a utopian dream that can never be realized. If you want to get ahead in this world, you've got to be practical and look out for Number One."

I mention this to show you that I know all the arguments against socialism. I heard them more than forty years ago. And I won't say that I didn't pay attention to them. I did. Especially the argument that socialism is a utopian dream that can never be realized. I was then, as I am now, inclined to realism, and I never saw any point in expending energy on impossible and unrealizable projects. The argument that socialism is not practical and not realizable worried me.

It was this troubled frame of mind that brought me, more than forty years ago, to an open forum such as this, conducted by the Socialist Educational Society in Kansas City. I went there in search of more detailed information about this thing called socialism, which had charmed me and inspired me with its grand promise of the future society of secure peace and abundance for all; a society based on equality, solidarity, and comradeship.

It was at that forum that I got my introduction to the ideas of Marx and Engels, the ideas of scientific socialism. From the discussions of that forum and the further study inspired by them, I became acquainted with Marx's analysis of capitalism, and his sweeping assertion that socialism is not only a good idea, but is the next inevitable stage of social evolution; that the further development of capitalism cannot lead to anything else but its downfall and the socialist reorganization of society.

That did it. That settled all my youthful doubts about practicality and realizability of the idea. It convinced me theoretically, and that is the firmest conviction there is, that all the forces of history were working on my side, on the side of socialism, and that all I had to do was lend a hand, along with others, to help the historic process along.

Compared to the privilege of participating in this magnificent historical mission, all the so-called practical concerns of life and the possible material rewards of conformity seemed trivial to me more than forty years ago, and they still do. I have never changed my mind about this question in all the intervening years. That was not because of dogmatic obstinacy, but simply because I saw no good reason to change my mind.

I have always been willing to listen to anybody who would undertake to explain or make an argument against socialism from a realistic, practical point of view. As I went along I continued to hear those arguments, and still hear them if I cock my ear in the direction of the most noise.

Every theory must be submitted to the test of events. That applies to the theory of Marxism, just as Marx ruthlessly applied it to all other theories. If I grew stronger in my socialist convictions as the years passed by, it was because it appeared to me that the development of events was confirming in life the analysis and predictions of Marx.

It was Marx himself who said that no social system can be superseded until it has exhausted its progressive capacities. If capitalism is capable of further progressive development on a world scale, and is therefore invulnerable against any attempts to change it in a radical manner, then there is not much point in arguing that socialism would be a better system.

But on the other hand, if capitalism has lost its progressive character and become reactionary, has ceased to grow and expand and develop the productive forces of the people, upon which all human welfare is based; if it has entered into its period of decline and decay—then the optimistic defenders of capitalism are in the wrong. They are the real utopians of the present day.

The issue, then, goes to the evidence, to the facts. Let us rest the case on this solid foundation of reality, and go to the facts as they have been unfolded in the great events of the past half century. If we look with clear eyes at what has already happened, we may get a good hint of what is going to happen. If we can see enough in these events to indicate a historical trend, then we can be fairly sure of what the ultimate outcome will be. It is by this method and from this point of view that I propose to discuss the international prospects of capitalism and socialism tonight. Naturally, in a single lecture, it will be possible to hit only the high spots, and I will confine my presentation to what I consider the six main facts of modern history.

It must be admitted that forty years ago there was some ground for the popular opinion that capitalism was a securely based, going concern, with a long life and few troubles ahead. Over a span of many decades, since 1871, the great powers had been at peace. Industry and trade had been expanding, the enslaved races in the colonies of Africa and Asia were being freely plundered without fear of revolts, and the workers in the advanced countries, partly sharing in the superprofits of the colonial plunder, enjoyed a small, but real, improvement in their standard of living. Democracy flourished.

Under such conditions there could be no prospect of a workers' revolution. Socialism was relegated to an ultimate goal whose realization was pushed far into the future. Marx's predictions about the increasing misery of the workers forcing them to revolution seemed to be refuted. The capitalists for their part, in those far-gone halcyon days, grew rich and complacent, fat and sassy and self-confident. With their trained economists at their elbows, they periodically raised their voices in a hearty and happy chorus of a song that might have been called: "Everything is Lovely and the Goose Hangs High."

Then something happened. Something went wrong. The world had suddenly grown too small for the rival capitalist powers in their mad scramble and competition for markets, colonial territories, and spheres of influence. The conflict suddenly exploded in 1914 in the First World War. This war, which lasted more than four years, cost 12 million dead and 20 million wounded, wrecked the economy of Europe, expanded the economy of America at the expense of Europe, raised America to first place among the imperialist powers, and, as a sort of by-product, resulted in the Russian Revolution, which tore one-sixth of the earth's surface out of the capitalist market.

This colossal shake-up, brought about by the First World War, can be put down under the head of *fact number one.* Quite a fact, you must admit, which looked bad for capitalism at the time, and has been getting worse ever since.

The war was a devastating blow to capitalism, at least as far as Europe was concerned. If its goose wasn't cooked, at least it didn't hang high any more.

America, remote from the scene of actual conflict, enriched itself on the spoils, but the world system had been irremediably dislocated. Its days of expansion were abruptly ended. In the postwar period the sleeping colonies began to stir. In the metropolitan centers of Europe the economy stagnated, and the living standards of the workers drastically declined. The war, and the terrible poverty resulting from it, radicalized the working masses of Europe, brought a revolution in Hungary, produced revolutionary situations in Italy and Germany, and put a question mark over the future prospects of capitalism as far as the whole of Europe was concerned. Europe, after the war, especially in Germany and Italy, was ripe for revolution. But the workers were not yet ready with a party that could lead it and carry it through. They paid dearly for that unpreparedness. The result was a series of defeats for the workers. And on the basis of these defeats, with the help of American loans, the capitalist economy in Europe slowly recovered and attained a new stabilization which brought new illusions of a new Golden Age of prosperity and expansion.

But no sooner was the new stabilization of the capitalist economy proclaimed and celebrated than the whole world was again shaken to its foundations by the world-wide economic crisis touched off by the New York stock market crash of 1929. This time rich and powerful America, which had grown fat at the expense of other countries in the war, was hit hardest of all. Production was cut in half, and the living standards of the workers were reduced in about the same measure. This crisis put an end to all prospect of capitalist expansion on the basis of stable, democratic regimes and brought fascism to power in poverty-stricken Germany following the earlier example of poverty-stricken Italy.

Just as the world war had put an end to capitalist prosperity based on peace, the 1929 crisis and its aftermath put an end to capitalist prosperity in Europe based on democracy.

The economic crisis of 1929, and the resort of capitalism in Italy and Germany to the monstrous crisis rule of fascism, can be put down as important *fact number two*. This was also bad for the prospects of capitalism, for it showed its economic system to be weakened, shaken and declining.

Meanwhile, earlier attempts of the great powers to overthrow the workers' government of the Soviet Union were defeated, the victory of the revolution was consolidated on the basis of national-ized and planned economy, with a monopoly of foreign trade. This closed off the Russian market to capitalist exploitation from abroad. During the crisis, which dragged on in the capitalist world for a number of years and was never really overcome, Russian industry under the five-year plans progressed by leaps and bounds, multi-plied its output many times and eventually brought the Soviet Union to second place in industrial production.

The survival of the Soviet Union in a hostile capitalist world, and its ability to increase and even multiply its productive capacity, while the economy of the capitalist countries was declining and stagnating, raises in the most striking and irrefutable fashion a hith-erto unproved assertion of Marxism: that is, the superiority as a productive force of a nationalized and planned economy—which is immune from crisis—over the anarchic, unplanned economy of capitalism, which cannot escape periodic crises. Here, in my opin-ion, is the key to the future development of the world.

This can be put down among our exhibits as *fact number three,* the fact which shows the rise and development of a new social and economic system simultaneously with capitalist decline.

By 1939, the basic conflicts which had caused the world war to break out in 1914 had not been eliminated. On the contrary, they reasserted themselves in a more aggravated form. Each one of the big powers, stifling in the still unresolved crisis which struck the capitalist world in 1929, saw its existence conditioned upon the ac-quisition and retention of foreign markets and territories and fields of influence for the export of its surplus goods and capital. The richer nations felt obliged to hang on to what outlets they had at all costs, and if possible to find new ones. German capitalism, on the other hand, defeated in the First World War, and suffocating in its restricted barriers, had to expand or perish. The same was true of Italy and Japan.

I think history will record the year 1939 as the fateful year of decision which finally sealed the fate of capitalism as a world system; the year in which terrible economic difficulties, brought about by the operation of the laws of capitalism, were supplemented and enormously aggravated by the bankruptcy of political and military decision. Capitalism lost the power to think for itself.

Here was the situation in 1939: The rival big powers of capitalism confronted each other as *rivals of the same kind, of the same system,* in the fight for a diminishing world market for trade and investment.

The Soviet Union, embracing one-sixth of the earth's surface, confronted all of them as a *rival of a different kind,* a rival representing a new and different social system, whose superiority over the social system of capitalism as a productive force had been demonstrated to the hilt in the prolonged crisis. The Soviet Union confronted the capitalist nations as a rival whose further existence and possible expansion could spell only death in the long run for the rival system of capitalism.

Moreover, the territory occupied by the Soviet Union had been withdrawn from the capitalist market since the revolution of 1917. And this fact in itself had contributed enormously to the economic difficulties of the capitalist nations, in Europe particularly.

It was the most imperative necessity of the capitalist nations in the fateful year of 1939 to take counsel together and to unite in their own enlightened self-interest, to face their greatest danger, which was at the same time their greatest opportunity. They were confronted with an overriding need to crush the Soviet Union and thereby to remove, for the time being at least, a rival social system from the world arena; and at the same time, to open up the Russian market for capitalist exploitation and thus get a new lease on life for the system as a whole.

The inability of the capitalist nations, because of conflict among themselves, to unite for this crucial and indispensable task in 1939, to save or at least to prolong their own life, was, in my opinion, the surest sign of their hopeless degeneration and decay, manifested by their inability even to think for themselves any longer.

It doesn't help matters any to say that it was all Hitler's fault and that Hitler was a madman. That is true enough. But what kind of social system is it when madmen can make its most important decisions? An historical law reasserted itself in this circumstance: the law that social systems which have outlived their time can't do anything right any longer.

Instead of uniting to attack the Soviet Union, the rival capitalist imperialist powers embarked upon a war among themselves. The Soviet Union was at first on the sidelines, and later engaged in the war with the powerful allies, America and Great Britain. The results of the war are well known. Germany and Japan, which previously had menaced the Soviet Union from the West and from the East, were crushed. The colonial and nationalist revolutions, taking advantage of the difficulties of the imperialist masters during the war, were able to strengthen their forces and undermine the whole colonial system, without which world capitalism cannot operate.

And on top of everything, the most important thing of all, the Soviet Union emerged victorious from the war and rose to the position of the first economic and military power in Europe.

Let us put all this down in our list of exhibits as *fact number four,* as a brightly lighted signpost pointing out the direction of future developments which were not long unfolding in the postwar period.

Formally speaking, the Axis powers—Germany, Italy, and Japan—lost the war, and the Allied powers, the United States, Britain, the Soviet Union, and France, won it. That's the way formal history records the outcome, and that's the way Churchill, the world's most articulate wishful thinker, writes it. The essential content within that outward form looks different. In reality, as measured by their actual position when the smoke cleared away, the Soviet Union and the United States emerged as the only victors and all the others were losers—England and France no less than Germany, Italy, and Japan.

After two victories in two world wars, Britain, once proud queen of the seas and banker of the world, ends up as a beggar, living on America's dole. Its days of glory have departed; its empire is shattered and falling apart, and all the king's horses and all the king's men can never put the jolly old empire together again.

France emerged from her victories in the two wars in the same position, only worse. The French empire is dying in agony on the battlefields of Indochina. Capitalist Britain and France are just a couple of American satellites.

The United States and the Soviet Union came out of the war as the only winners—with one important qualification: the colonial world rose to its feet during the war and entered the arena of world history as an independent force. The course of history in the postwar period has been primarily determined by the relations between these three powers, the United States, the Soviet Union, and the insurgent colonial world. All the other countries play merely supporting roles.

America's position in the new world setup is a truly great one. Let no patriotic vigilante accuse me of minimizing it. I admit it, even if I'm not proud of it. The United States is the first and dominant power of the entire capitalist world, economically and militarily. It has the money and the bombs and the moral self-satisfaction too. What could be cozier than that? Our boys in Wall Street are doing all right for themselves. They don't even have to play a fiddle. All they have to do is whistle, and the others dance. But—and here we come to the fly in our ointment, or maybe it is somebody's thumb in our eye—that section of the world which is no longer capitalist, or is trying to break away from capitalism, doesn't want to dance to America's tune. A conflict over this matter has been in progress ever since the end of the war.

An examination of the course this conflict is taking is now pertinent to the question posed in the subject of our discussion: "The International Prospects of Capitalism and Socialism." The question might be put in another way: "Who is winning the cold war?" The question could be formulated in a third way and be even more precise: "Is revolution and the nationalization of industry, the economic foundation for socialism and the transition to it, gaining ground, or being pushed back?"

The answer to the riddle of the future is wrapped up in this formulation of the question. Obviously, America has been losing the first rounds. That's bad enough; the odds at the ringside always turn against a fighter who has to come from behind. But if our examination shows that America has not only been losing ground but is the chief author of its own setbacks, the odds on the final outcome must be changed radically. No fighter is so sure to lose as the one who knocks himself out. And that, my friends—candor obliges me to report—is precisely what our great and glorious country—or more correctly, the Wall Street people who own this country lock, stock, and barrel—is doing in the battle for the championship of the world.

I charge them with throwing the fight. I accuse them before the Un-American Activities Committee, on my oath and without claiming any rights against self-incrimination—I accuse the Wall Street money sharks as the world's greatest and most dangerous revolutionists, as the chief instigators of social revolution, colonial revolt, and nationalization of industry in the entire world.

Look what they have done in Eastern Europe. This territory wasn't "given away to the Russians at Yalta," as the irresponsible radicals on the lunatic fringe of the Republican Party say. It was simply a power vacuum filled by the Red Army as a result of its victory and the collapse of the Nazi war machine. Predominant Soviet influence in this territory was an ineluctable circumstance resulting from the war.

The question was how to accommodate this circumstance to the interests of American and world capitalism. Stalin, for his part, was willing to make such an accommodation. He offered, and in good faith too, to maintain and guarantee the capitalist system of production and the capitalist form of government in the countries of Eastern Europe. And that is precisely what he did in the first three years of the postwar period. He went further and offered to guarantee the capitalist system of production and capitalist political regimes in Italy and France, where they were badly shaken.

And that is precisely what he did there too, by sending Communist Party representatives into the bourgeois cabinets as supporting forces. Their special assignment was to curb the workers and suppress strikes, and they carried it out. In return for these truly great concessions to prop up the tottering system of capitalism in both Western and Eastern Europe, Stalin asked only a small concession in return—a deal.

"Let us alone in our part of the world," he said in effect, "and we will let you alone in your part. Let's coexist and be happy."

But the rulers of America said, "No." Drunk with power and ignorance, combined perhaps with that senile dementia which invariably strikes the ruling circles of outlived social systems, they decided to "get tough with Russia." They responded to Stalin's conciliatory policy in Eastern Europe with a stepped-up armaments program and the Marshall Plan.

The Marshall Plan was contrived to let America's stricken Allies in Europe live, or rather breathe, while strengthening America's grip on their economy. At the same time it was designed to break the economies of the Eastern European countries out of the orbit of Soviet trade and harness them to the West. The Stalinists replied (they had no alternative) by breaking up the bourgeois governments in Eastern Europe—they were so weak, lacking all popular support, that they could be dismissed by a mere police action—and proceeding to the nationalization of the industries.

This was nothing less than an economic revolution, instigated by America and carried out by bureaucratic means. In France and Italy the Communist Party representatives were kicked out of the cabinets at the behest of the American paymaster. The Stalinists responded—again they had no alternative—by switching to a policy of opposition and radical agitation.

These are tremendous developments of world-historical import. The extension of the system of nationalized and planned economy—not socialism, but the economic foundation for it—to the whole of Eastern Europe means and can mean nothing else than the exclusion of this whole territory from the world capitalist market and a consequent shrinking of the capitalist sector of world economy, which is already too small. The ouster of the Stalinists from the governments of Italy and France means and can mean nothing else than a stimulus to the radicalization of the working class in these two decisive nations.

Let us put down these colossal happenings, loaded with revolutionary dynamite, as *fact number five,* and ascribe the main responsibility to the revolutionary incendiaries of New York and Washington. "Father, forgive them, they know not what they do." That's the way it reads in the Bible, but history will not be so magnanimous.

The camera eye now shifts to China and the colonial world. And what a world of unexpected wonders and calamities, with signs and portents of more to come, it has turned out to be. American capitalism went fishing in the Orient and caught a whale big enough to sink the boat. The war in the Orient was fought over China. It was fought by America in the name of the noblest ideals enunciated by Roosevelt, the greatest enunciator of them all.

The declared aim of the war was to drive the Japanese imperialists out of China and liberate this great country of half a billion people; to secure for China, by the armed might of magnanimous America, an independent, prosperous national existence, free from all foreign domination and exploitation.

That's one way of explaining our war aims, anyway. Another way would be to say that America waged the war in the Orient to drive the Japanese out of China, and get this tremendous market, the richest prize in all the world, for itself, for its own unhampered exploitation. That would be a more accurate way of putting it.

The development of China on a basis of capitalist economy, with a stable government capable of guaranteeing the eventual repayment of loans and credits, could have provided America with an outlet for its huge surpluses of goods and capital for years to come. And if the other capitalist powers were allowed to participate, even modestly, in the exploitation of this almost limitless market, they also might have overcome their internal crises and attained a new stabilization of their systems, also, for a period of years to come.

From a strictly capitalist standpoint, one must admit that such a prospect was well worth a war, even without any moralistic pretensions. And if the enterprise could be dressed up with idealistic bunkum at no extra cost, all the better. Anyway, we fought the war with Japan over China.

And the first half of the war aims were realized completely. Japan was driven out of China by military force, and even driven out of its other possessions, and condemned to stifle and stagnate in its own little chain of islands. But again something happened. Again something went wrong. America had staked all its cards on Chiang Kai-shek, the political and military leader of capitalist China. It allied itself with him and the narrow stratum of capitalists, landlords, and usurers whom he represented, and overlooked the Chinese people, who number half a billion, most of them hungry for land and bread.

These hungry people, just when the first half of the American plans were executed, with the defeat of Japan, most inconsiderately decided to get Chiang Kai-shek and his parasitic gang off their necks along with the Japanese. They started a ruckus, otherwise known as a revolutionary civil war. Chinese capitalism, deformed in its development by colonial exploitation of the great powers, had become senile before it reached maturity, senile, weak, corrupt, and parasitical.

The Chinese capitalist government of Chiang Kai-shek, propped up by American money and military support, and without much else to lean on, was not strong enough to contend with the popular revolt. By 1948 the popular revolution had driven Chiang Kai-shek and his gang completely off the mainland of China.

And one bright day the world was suddenly confronted with a new China, which was really independent, but backward in its industrial development and eager to get foreign loans and credits. The government of Mao Tse-tung offered to guarantee the capitalist system of production and to guarantee all loans on that basis.

The statesmen and leaders of British capitalism, who are older, wiser, and more experienced in world affairs, wanted to come to terms with the new reality, to recognize the new revolutionary government and continue trading with the new China. But the American statesmen and leaders wouldn't have it that way. They can't understand how it happened. They feel that somebody gypped them, and they are as indignant as a farmer who has been played for a sucker in a carnival shell game. China, according to their thinking, "belongs" to them and somehow or other, by some trick or other, they "lost" it.

That was a literal statement, repeated a thousand times in the recent election campaign: "We lost China." But did this great nation, with its half billion people and its unmeasured natural riches, really "belong" to them? Did Santa Claus promise them China for Christmas and then fail to deliver? Did somebody shoot Santa Claus? That's what they seem to think. Anyway that's the way they carry on in their mad search for spies and other culprits in the State Department.

As for China itself, they arrogantly ordered the revolutionary seas to subside; continued to bet their money on Chiang Kai-shek, the horse that had already lost the race; refused recognition to the new revolutionary Chinese government; refused them the loans and credits they were eager to get and to make concessions for; and established a virtual blockade against any foreign trading with China.

What are the results of all this wisdom? We can list the three most important ones: First, American policy alienated the sympathies of hundreds of millions of people throughout the Orient and the whole colonial world who had previously taken our idealistic pretensions in good faith. Revolts and revolutions throughout the entire colonial world, starting in Asia, then spreading to the Middle East, then to Africa, and now already leaping across to South America, are being fed today by hatred of American imperialism as gasoline feeds a fire.

The Korean War is a part of the colonial revolution. That's why it has presented so many surprises to the arrogant American militarists. The power of hunger is behind these revolutions—hunger for bread and land and national independence—and no power on earth can stop them.

The second result of America's policy of refusing to recognize the new Chinese government, refusing to trade with it, ordering a blockade against it, and even threatening war against it—the second result of this policy is to close off all possibilities of any further development of China on the basis of capitalist economy. Regardless of what their intentions and wishes might be, the Chinese Stalinists at the head of the new revolutionary government will be forced, as were the regimes in Eastern Europe, to embark on a wholesale program of nationalization, as a condition for the survival and development of the country's economy.

China couldn't be developed on a capitalist basis without a tremendous influx of foreign capital in the form of loans, credits, and investments. Deprived of this blood transfusion, weak, undeveloped, and shaken, Chinese capitalism—whatever may be left of it at this moment—is condemned to die of anemia. It has to be put out of its misery as the precondition for the revival and development of Chinese industry and agriculture.

If one is willing to recognize reality, regardless of what his personal wishes might be, he can safely predict that China will witness the development of a nationalization program on an ever-expanding basis, bringing with it an expansion of that sector of world economy held by nationalized and planned economy, and shrinking further that section held by capitalist economy.

The Wall Street financiers who shudder at modest welfare benefits in America as a form of "creeping socialism" are, by their policy, instigating and forcing a galloping program of nationalization of industry in China, which, I repeat again, is not socialism, but the economic preparation and premises for it and the transition to it.

A third result of America's arbitrary policy of blockading China and refusing to allow other capitalist nations to trade with her is the powerful blow it deals British capitalism. At a time when the very existence of capitalist Britain depends on an expansion of its foreign trade, America's policy in China arbitrarily drives it from the Chinese market. Thereby they worsen the already helpless position of British capitalist economy, undermine the living standards of the British workers, and drive them to Bevanism on the road to Bolshevism.

Blindly, unconsciously, but all the more surely and effectively, the masters of America are doing Lenin's work in Merry England. The disciples of Lenin, from London to Los Angeles to Shanghai and all points in between, should recognize the extraordinary help they are getting from the leaders and masters of American capitalism, even if they feel no need to express their gratitude formally.

The Chinese revolution, America's policy toward it, and the catastrophic results of this policy can be put down as the *sixth and final outstanding fact* in our panoramic survey of world developments over the past half century.

Whatever side one may take in this worldwide struggle between capitalism and socialism, anyone with a respect for facts must recognize that enough important facts have been piled up in the course of world development since 1914 to indicate an unmistakable trend. That trend shows capitalist economy ridden everywhere by incurable crisis, declining and decaying.

On the other hand, the historical trend shows the sector of nationalized economy expanding, an increasing radicalization of the workers in the crisis-ridden countries of capitalist Europe, and a veritable prairie fire of colonial revolutions breaking out everywhere and increasing in power and intensity all the time. The masters of America, the financial overlords and the political spokesmen all together, see these facts and these trends as well as we do.

They have but one answer. That is counterrevolution by military force. They propose to reverse the historic trend by another war. This is what they are preparing for; this is what they are trying to drag their reluctant allies into. The satellite governments of England, France, and Italy will be the allies of American imperialism in this terrible, desperate adventure of a third world war. The thin stratum of landlords, capitalists, and usurers in the backward countries will be their allies too.

But that is just about all they can count on. The majority of the people in Europe, including England, are outspokenly neutral or hostile to America. Where, then, will the troops come from? America is rich and powerful, the most productive nation in the world, with 160 million people. That is a tremendous power. But the two billion people in the world are a still bigger power. And when you contemplate the possible or probable outcome of the war and weigh the forces and resources on each side, don't forget to count the two billion people in the world. They could be, and, in my opinion, will be, the item which tips the scales and decides the outcome.

There is no doubt whatsoever, and no one who has respect for facts can deny it, that the prospects for capitalism on an international scale, outside the United States, are bad and declining. The prospects for nationalized economy and the further spread of radicalization and revolution are ascending. That's the state of the world as it looks from here.

But what about America itself? Capitalism is certainly supreme here, and socialism is very weak indeed. It is reduced to a virtual handful of people with a theory and conviction. What are the prospects between these two antagonists within the United States?

That, as Kipling would say, is another story, and we'll get around to it next week.

Prospects of capitalism and socialism in America

America is no longer an island, sheltered and protected by two ocean barriers. America today is involved in the world. After all that has happened in modern times, especially since 1914, and particularly since the Second World War, it is pretty generally understood by all except a few Republican dinosaurs, that American isolationism has no basis in modern reality.

The late Wendell Willkie is chiefly remembered for his sudden discovery and excited announcement that we live in "One World." That is true in more senses than one, and was known even before Willkie made a trip to foreign lands and discovered that the great globe itself is really "round and firm and fully packed," even if it isn't "free and easy on the draw."[*]

We do, indeed, live in one world in which no nation can any longer be an island to itself. But for the purposes of this discussion, I have temporarily, but only temporarily, and for convenience in the discussion, divided the world into two parts, the United States and the rest of the world.

---

[*] A reference to a familiar cigarette commercial of the time.

Last week we discussed the prospects of capitalism and socialism in the world at large, outside the borders of our own country. This week we examine the prospects of these two rival and irreconcilable social systems in the United States itself.

The picture here, at least as it appears at first sight, is quite different in many respects. The United States is rich and prosperous, while the majority of the people in the rest of the world never get enough to eat.

Politically, the United States is conservative, even reactionary, and turning even further to the right, as shown by the Republican victory in the recent election. Throughout the rest of the world, from Europe to the Orient, the political trend is unmistakably to the left.

In the United States the capitalist system of production is strong and apparently secure. The same economic system in the rest of the world is obviously in a state of permanent crisis, declining and decaying, and in one sector after another giving way before the system of nationalized industry and planned economy, the material foundation and transitional stage to socialism.

From the looks of things, again as they appear at first glance, the United States and the rest of the world are traveling in opposite directions, and can never meet and join together. That, however, is an optical illusion. The two parts of one world are indissolubly bound together and the stronger part will unfailingly drag the other part along.

Last week we proved and rested our case on a mass of known facts which unmistakably demonstrate the decline and decay of the capitalist system and the historical trend toward socialism in the rest of the world. The same case, in my opinion, can be proved in the United States. But here our approach is necessarily more theoretical.

And by theoretical, I don't mean "impractical" or visionary. I don't mean to disregard facts, but simply to put them in place. I propose to take the known facts in their interrelationship, trace them to their origin and consider them as elements in a process, and thus to bring out their full implications. By this theoretical method—it is the method of Marxism—of relating facts to each other and disclosing their implications, I will undertake to prove that America is no privileged "exception" and can by no means resist the pull of the historical tide.

Not only is socialism a possible outcome of the development of capitalism in the United States, it is the historically necessary and inevitable outcome.

Indeed, the very strength of American capitalism at the present moment, and its great victories and achievements of the past, will appear and be recognized in history as contributions to American socialism, preparing the material conditions and foundation for it, and making the socialist victory certain. Furthermore, the victory of socialism in the United States is not an ultimate goal of the far-off misty future. It is the perspective of the present epoch.

The United States, from its beginning, has been the luckiest and most favored of all capitalist nations. And thanks to the wisdom of its founders, and their continuators in its first century, it played its luck for all it was worth.

The thirteen original colonies started off with a thoroughgoing revolution which secured their independence, and thus freed the country from the foreign exploitation and political control which restricted and deformed the economic development of colonial lands such as India and China.

Our country, from the beginning, was also free from outlived feudal obstructions which hampered and restricted the free development of capitalism in Europe for decades and generations, and which, in some countries, persist even to this day.

In addition, thanks to its political centralization under one federal government, its economy was able to develop as a single unit over a vast territory, without customs barriers and expensive armies to guard them between the states; while Europe, due to historical conditions, is even today split up into a score or more of separate states, competing with each other, armed against each other, and jealously guarding their borders against the free flow of trade and commerce.

The centralized, single government created by the founding fathers gave, and continues to give, the United States of America great economic advantages over the disunited states of Europe.

Finally, thanks to the revolution, the United States began with a bourgeois-democratic form of government without any monarchical trappings whatever; the very best arena for the free development of capitalism in its ascending stage.

The most fortunate nations are those which have their social revolutions when they are due. America owes its greatness as an economic power, not merely to one revolution, but to two, and both of them arrived on time. When the time had come for America's first revolution, it was carried through to the end by a resolute leadership. The second American revolution also came in time, and there was no fooling this time, either.

The antiquated and inefficient economy based on slave labor had survived the first American revolution in the Southern states and tried to extend itself to the new territories being opened up. Slavery as an economic system stood as a barrier in the way of the development of the more efficient system of capitalist production based on wage labor. Moreover, the attempted secession of the Southern slave states threatened to break up the political unity of the country and fragment it along European lines. This issue, properly described by Seward as the "irrepressible conflict," was also resolved in a thoroughgoing manner by the Civil War of 1861–65, which was also a social revolution, and a most beneficent one, too.

After some preliminary political fumbling and military indecisiveness on the part of generals who didn't know what the war was about, Lincoln issued the Emancipation Proclamation, and found a general to implement it. The Southern Confederacy, and with it the whole economic system based on chattel slavery, was hammered into dust by the iron fist of Grant.

The Civil War, America's second revolution, guaranteed the national unity of the states under one federal government and extended its domain from border to border and from coast to coast. Thus the political prerequisite for the unhampered development of the entire continent as one economic unit was secured for American capitalism by two revolutions.

Why, then, should we throw fits over the word? That shows disrespect for the history of our country, or ignorance of it. We are where we are, and what we are, because of two revolutions.

If the United States as a nation was born under the lucky star of one revolution, and had its political unity secured by another, its development and expansion as a capitalist economic power was also favored above all others by geographic factors. These, in simple modesty we ought to admit, were not invented by the genius of American capitalism, but were laid in its lap as a gift of nature.

The new nation was also favored by the contradictions of European economy, which, operating blindly, as is the law of capitalism, aided its American rival to expand and eventually to become its master.

Expansion is the law of life for the capitalist system of economy. The profits extracted by the exploitation of wage labor must be invested in new fields. The surplus produce which the capitalists and their retainers can't consume and the workers can't buy, must be sold in other markets. New territory, new markets—that's what capitalism wants for Christmas every day of the year, and runs into trouble if it doesn't get it.

American capitalism, emerging from the Civil War with a unified country, found these new territories and markets right in its own back yard. It found a whole continent, larger in area than the European heartland of capitalism in the nineteenth century; larger than all of continental Western Europe, plus England, Ireland, Scotland and Wales, and the islands of the Hebrides. American capitalism found a continent fabulously rich in fertile lands, plus coal, iron, timber, oil, metal—all the natural resources necessary for an expanding economy. And it was all their own. Their exclusive right and title to it was copyrighted in all languages, including the Scandinavian.

The geographical position of American capitalism gave it great advantages over its European rivals and guaranteed its victory over them in the long run. While the European states, stifling within their restricted national barriers, were compelled to find markets for their surplus goods, sources of raw materials, and fields of investment for their surplus capital in foreign lands, America had these markets and territories right at home, right in its own back yard. For decade after decade the ever-expanding frontier was pushed westward, and each new territory opened up became a new field for investment and a new market for surplus goods produced in the East.

In their insatiable hunt for raw materials and markets for their finished goods, as well as for the investment of their surplus capital, the European countries embarked on a vast program of colonial conquest. America's colonies were right at home in the newly opened territories on the frontier. They were richer, and yielded better returns; and they had the additional advantage of an internal river and lakes system that made transportation even cheaper than the sea lanes tying the old empires together, and no large standing armies were required to conquer and pacify them and keep them in subjection.

In this respect America had all the advantages in a material sense, plus the added virtue of appearing as the champion of national independence, with no interest in the acquisition of colonies. This combination of big profits and virtue which costs nothing appealed powerfully to the Yankee sense of moral values, if not to its sense of humor.

America differed, to its advantage, from Europe in another way. While Europe was plagued with mass unemployment, causing all kinds of social unrest, the expanding American frontiers continuously drained off the surplus labor power in the cities and provided many opportunities, unknown in Europe, for workers to rise out of the proletarian class and become small farmers or businessmen. At the same time, the relative labor shortage improved the position of the American workers in the labor market and compelled the employers to pay higher wages than were paid to the workers of Europe.

The net result of all this was to slow down the development of class consciousness, to cut the ground from beneath a radical and socialist labor movement and to assure the political stability of the bourgeois regime in the United States. At the same time, the labor movement of Europe, where class divisions were firmly fixed, was growing and developing along socialist lines.

Capitalist Europe helped capitalist America to expand and develop in still another way—by exporting great masses of surplus workers and farmers. They came to the new land in succeeding waves of millions upon millions to supply the skill and manpower to build up the great new country: skilled workers from England, the original workshop of the world; German mechanics and farmers; Irish and Italian laborers; Jews and other refugees from Poland and Russia; and later, great waves of South Slavs, and others from the countries of Eastern Europe.

They came in their millions to America, as immigrants, to do the hard and dirty work of building up the country and piling up the profits of its owners. Asia, too, helped in this respect. The Union Pacific Railroad, for example, from California to Promontory Point, Utah, where the Golden Spike was driven to celebrate the first union of the entire continent by rail, was built by Chinese laborers with their picks and shovels, in the same way they are building new railroads in the new China today.

The relative shortage of labor which compelled the American capitalists to pay higher wages than the capitalists of Europe—as much as two and three times higher in some cases—was turned into an advantage for the development of American industry. It compelled and stimulated the introduction of labor-saving machinery and all the modern processes of increasing the productivity of labor while reducing the labor force.

Finally, and perhaps most important of all, European capitalism stimulated and helped the hothouse growth and expansion of its American rival by huge investments of its surplus capital. The building of the American railroad system, for example, was financed mainly by English capital; Holland, France, Switzerland, and Germany also contributed a considerable volume.

So, in summing things up, with due regard to the facts, we ought to admit, in all frankness, that the prodigious growth of the American economic giant, until it grew bigger than all others and overshadowed all others, was not entirely due to the genius of American businessmen and bankers. Two revolutions were the starting impulsion. Great natural and geographic advantages provided the arena. The political and economic disunity of Europe gave America another advantage. European capital investments speeded up the construction of the greatest enterprises. And European labor provided a great deal of the skill and elbow grease to build up the industry and agriculture of this country.

European capitalism did all this blindly, not with any good intentions, but because it couldn't help itself, and therefore deserves no special gratitude. But the rich American capitalists really shouldn't begrudge the few billions in loans and gifts which they are now handing out to Europe as a beggar's dole. Charity is doubly sweet to the donor when it can be bestowed on a former benefactor at a big discount.

Along about the turn of the century, America's conquest of its own continent was just about completed and there was no place else to go. Father Neptune drew a line at the water's edge of the Pacific and said, "You can't go any further here." The free land was gone, and all the new territories were pretty well settled up. The problem of new markets for the ever-increasing surpluses, piled up by the ever-increasing productivity of American labor, was becoming Problem No. 1.

In 1907 there was a crisis. And again in 1914 there was mounting unemployment. It was then that the European capitalist nations, America's perennial Santa Claus, once again came to the rescue of the American economy. They involved themselves in a destructive war over markets, colonies, spheres of influence and fields of investment, and America warmed its hands by the fire. Remaining benevolently neutral on the side of the Allies for the first three years of the war, America found in the war itself the richest market it could ever have dreamed of.

While the normal peacetime economy of the Western Allies was dislocated by the war, American factories worked overtime to supply their deficiencies. America was still a debtor nation when the war started, but the huge purchases which France and England were compelled to make in America soon canceled out all indebtedness. America emerged as a creditor nation, even before the war was over.

At the same time, while the Western Allies and Germany were busy in their life-and-death battle, America obligingly edged them out of the South American market. This provided another outlet for the endless supply of goods rolling from the assembly lines in all kinds of factories from one end of the United States to another.

So great were the demands of the war in Europe, for goods and materials, that America was obliged to expand its productive plant, and thereby its productive capacities, to supply them. When America, after a hugely profitable delay of three years, finally entered the war in order to protect her loans to the Allied powers, she only had to tip the scales a bit to finish off the Kaiser's army.

Comparatively speaking, America was scarcely touched by the war, in terms of casualties, and was enormously enriched by it in economic and financial terms. Exhausted Europe emerged from the war as America's debtor and dependent, and has remained in that position, under increasingly degrading conditions, ever since.

The First World War brought America to the position of leading power in the capitalist world, having no further need of any more capital investments from Europe, or any more of Europe's manpower. Since then, America has been concerned only with the problem of propping up Europe with loans, sufficient to enable it to ward off collapse and the danger of revolution, without allowing it to enter the world market again as a real competitor. Capitalist America, the beneficiary in its youth of the aid of capitalist Europe, became in the period of its maturity the ungrateful nemesis of this same Europe.

The impoverishment of Europe, rendered permanent by the economic and financial domination of the United States, deprives it of any further prospect of expansion on a capitalist basis. Therewith, the living standards of the European workers are degraded and they are pushed on the road of radicalization and revolution.

America's progress up to the First World War had been steadily upward along a straight line, with no serious complications. The American capitalists, who were the beneficiaries of all this historical luck, imagined themselves to be the authors of it. Everything had seemed simple. All you had to do was to open up new territories, increase production and get richer, and everything else would be added unto you.

As long as things worked out that way, they saw no need of theory, no need of philosophy, no need to bother about the rest of the world. But with the outcome of the First World War, and the chronic impoverishment of Europe, the complications for America began. Isolationism, which up to then had been the almost universal American doctrine, was called into question by some of the bourgeois political thinkers, notably by Woodrow Wilson.

It was becoming clear to them that America's rise to the position of first power in the world, involved it in all the affairs of the world. The United States was no longer isolated and alone, secure on an island protected by two oceans. Its investments and its interests extended all over the capitalist world, and all the crises and revolutionary disturbances in any part of the world became lodged in America's own foundations.

There was one historically brief period, however, when all that was forgotten, when all America, capitalists, middle class, and workers alike, relaxed in carefree optimism. That was the period of the Great American Boom of the postwar period, in the twenties.

The increase in foreign trade, the yawning foreign market for American capital in the form of loans and investments, which were freely supplied from America with the naive confidence that they would surely be returned with big interest (nobody had told them that nations as well as business firms can go bankrupt); the accumulated demands in the building industry which had piled up during the war, and other demands of the internal market, including the great new demand for automobiles and agricultural machinery—all this provided the conditions for a prosperity which soon reached the proportions of a boom.

Pragmatism, that peculiar and distinctive American philosophy, the philosophy of no philosophy, which recognizes nothing that it cannot see, and considers what it sees as fixed and final, had a final fling in the fantastic boom days of the 1920s. With the exception of a handful of Marxists, who considered facts of the day from the point of view of how they began, and in what direction they were moving, the American people—capitalists, college professors, middle class, and workers—indulged themselves in an orgy of faith: faith in the fantastic delusion that American business genius had solved the problem of permanent prosperity.

The sober analysis and conclusions of Marx, dealing with reality as it is in process, and not merely as it appears at the moment, became the object of refutation and ridicule by all kinds of theoretical triflers and economic smart alecks and pipsqueaks. Marx said history is a process of social evolution preparing a new form of social organization. But Henry Ford said, "History is bunk," and that struck the popular note. "Karl Marx is dead! Long Live Henry Ford!" That's what they were all shouting, in effect, on the very day the boom blew up in the stock-market crash on a damp October day in 1929.

The stock-market crash and the ensuing crisis showed that facts are not always what they look like, standing alone. They are the outcome of preceding facts and also causative factors of new changes in a continuous process.

The crisis of the thirties demonstrated that American capitalist economy has no immunity from the laws which govern the same capitalist economy in other countries; that if its crises had been deferred by exceptionally favorable factors in the past, it was only to accumulate the material for a more powerful explosion when it came. The contradictions of capitalism simply caught up with its favored American sector and made it pay double for the delay. The crisis put a question mark over the future of American capitalism and made the American people crisis conscious and fearful of the future. The old confidence in the future of capitalism and the feeling of security had gone with the wind.

The crisis of 1929, which lasted ten years, with some ups and downs within the crisis, was never solved except by the artificial means of expenditures for war and armaments. That was no solution, it was only a postponement. The unsolved crisis was still latent in the American economy after the end of World War II and was making its way ominously to the surface, when the huge new armaments program of the cold war again pushed it back. But the crisis is still there, still latent, silently growing like a malignant cancer in the body of American economy.

Can expenditures for armaments, and even for war, provide a permanent cure for the sick economy whose expanded productive forces collide against a shrinking market in a shrinking capitalist world? Can America provide the conditions of permanent prosperity which will moderate the class struggle at home and prevent the development of a determined class consciousness on the part of the working class, and thereby secure for itself a long and stable existence? Or do all the signs prove the opposite?

These are questions which even the most foolhardy bourgeois economists, after the catastrophe of their prophecies in the previous boom period, hesitate to answer. The best they will say is, "It looks all right for the time being, but we don't know all the facts and can't tell what's going to be."

We Marxists, on the other hand, say we know the facts. At least we know enough of them, and the general direction of their development, to tell what is going to be. And on this solid basis of facts in their process of development, we confidently assert that American capitalism has already passed the peak of its development and has no place to go from now on, but down. The historical luck of American capitalism is running out. All those factors which favored its development from the beginning, cushioned the shocks of cyclical crises, and enabled it to grow at the expense of other capitalist nations, are either exhausted or turning into their opposites.

The internal market has reached the saturation point, and cannot be further extended. The frontier territories, which once absorbed huge amounts of surplus goods and capital, are long since settled up and fully developed, and most of them now produce their own surpluses. Our own state of California is a shining example of a former "importer" becoming an "exporter."

Any prospect of stabilizing the American economy on the basis of its internal market is absolutely excluded. Increased foreign trade, won by the United States as a result of the First World War, helped to spark the great economic boom of the twenties. But now, the world market, which America dominates as a result of its economic preponderance and the bankruptcy of its rivals, no longer offers an adequate outlet for America's glut of capital and surplus goods.

To be sure, the backward countries need what America produces to excess, but they can't pay for it. That difficulty might be overcome by loans and credits if these countries had stable bourgeois governments which the United States could trust to guarantee eventual payment. But there are very few such governments left in the world, and their number is decreasing.

The advanced industrial countries, on the other hand, need to increase their own exports. They not only need to share in the world market, where America crowds them out, but also want access to the American market, which America bars by tariffs. The domination of the world market, which America fell heir to in the epoch of capitalist decline, offers no solution of her economic problem.

Of the various factors which once contributed to the rise and expansion of American capitalism, there remains only the factor of revolution which provided its first big impulsion. Revolutions of the same kind are still taking place in the world, and American capitalism is partly responsible for them, but is not benefited by them. By its greedy, monopolistic, and reactionary policy, it helps to ruin the economy of other countries, and drive the people to revolution. Then it tries to stop the revolutions with money, guns, and bombs.

They act something like a schizophrenic fireman I once heard of, who was also a pyromaniac. He ran himself ragged all day trying to put out the fires he had started the night before. He never could catch up with his work.

America's schizophrenic policy of revolution and counterrevolution is a hopeless undertaking. Revolution, the benevolent friend of American capitalism in its infancy and surging adolescence, has become its mortal enemy in its twilight years. All the old avenues of expansion and development are closed off. The American capitalist economy is in a blind alley. There is no way out.

From these economic facts we conclude that American capitalism is doomed, and that socialism will take its place. This transformation, of course, will not take place automatically. A little political action will be required. But the economic facts we have summarized are preparing all the conditions for this political action and will generate all the necessary forces to assure its success.

The victory of Socialist America is already written in the stars.

The coming struggle for power

Our subject tonight, "The Coming Struggle for Power," refers to the showdown struggle between the workers and the capitalists to decide who shall be master in the American house. Is it looking too far ahead to put this question up for discussion now? I don't think so.

I know that many people can't see this coming struggle for power in our land, because immediate indications are not observable to them. They see what's happened in the rest of the world, but imagine that America has some special immunity. They are profoundly mistaken. The workers' revolution is on the historical agenda in the United States, and not too far down on the agenda at that.

Everybody knows that the rest of the world is badly shaken up. Hardly a week goes by but a new country swims into the headlines with the announcement of a new crisis, or a revolution, or something of that sort. For the past couple of weeks the Allied world has been agonizing with France, over the crisis in the French cabinet. If my recollection is correct, that particular crisis was solved the other day, if it hasn't broken loose again since the evening papers went to press.

We take it for granted that the whole world is in crisis and up-heaval; the evidence is there for all to see. But here in the United States, in this land especially favored by superior virtues, by luck, or as some may say, by Providence, we are reminded that nothing of the kind is happening. That's true. It is also said that it can't happen here. That's not so true.

On the surface everything looks good for the ruling monopo-lists. In contrast to all the rest of the world, social relations in the United States alone appear to be stable. There's no crisis. No real upsurge in the class struggle. Not even serious strikes. The recent elections gave convincing proof of this social stability at the mo-ment. There was no challenge to the rule of the bourgeoisie in the last election. In fact, big capital felt so sure of itself that it could dispense with the Democratic-labor coalition which had governed America—for the benefit of big capital—for the past twenty years. The monopolists felt such firm ground beneath their feet in this country—not in the rest of the world, but here—that they could dispense with the political regime of twenty years, the regime which in part had leaned on the support and cooperation of the orga-nized labor movement. They stepped forward to rule directly in their own name. That was the meaning of the Eisenhower victory. And as you have observed the appointments of Eisenhower to his cabinet, you can see that they have dared to construct their gov-ernment on the narrowest class basis ever in the history of this country.

The *New Republic*, in the last few weeks, has been running a se-ries of biographical sketches of the multimillionaires who have been selected to sit in Eisenhower's cabinet, where the great deci-sions will be made. He has dispensed with second-rate business-men and even with first-rate businessmen, to say nothing of hack politicians, and has stacked his cabinet with the direct represen-tatives of the biggest capital concentrations in the country. All multimillionaires or lawyers for multimillionaires, plus one cap-tive labor skate sitting meekly in a corner like the king's fool in a medieval court. Durkin* is there strictly for laughs.

The *New York Post* financial editor observed that "this is not Big Business running the government; this is Big Big Business." Another paper reported an interview with one of the top financial magnates of the country about the "millionaires' cabinet" selected by Eisenhower. He said, "It looks very good, and I hope it works; but sometimes I'm scared."

He may well be "scared," for this present stability rests on world foundations which are by no means firm. This forebodes great and even rapid changes in the whole situation. America's social stability of the moment occurs in the midst of a world torn and shaken by crises and revolutions and wars and rumors of war. And now that America has become the master of the capitalist world, her foundations are extended over all these volcanoes, exploding or about to explode in all parts of what is left of the capitalist world.

It is utterly utopian, in my opinion, to expect that the present stability in one country alone can endure. The very narrow class base of the Eisenhower regime will make it more vulnerable, deprive it of cushions and shock supports, such as the Roosevelt and Truman administrations had in their alliance with the labor bureaucracy and its consequent support of the official policy.

A social crisis in this country is certain. As a matter of fact, a social crisis, as I view it, is already in the making. The unsolved crisis of the thirties, only artificially suppressed by the device of war and armaments expenditures of many hundreds of billions of dollars; the whole world situation—all things conspire together to generate a social crisis capable of exploding far sooner than the wise men dream.

The social convulsion can begin as an economic crisis even before the war, if for some reason they find it necessary or expedient

---

* Martin P. Durkin, president of the AFL Plumbers Union, was appointed secretary of labor by Eisenhower in his first cabinet. Durkin resigned after eight months in office, claiming Eisenhower had reneged on an agreement to send "pro-labor" amendments to the Taft-Hartley Act to Congress.

to postpone the outbreak of a third world war. In the year 1953, they will be running right up against the fact that, with a military budget of 60 billion dollars a year, they are just barely keeping the economic equilibrium. The slightest slacking off of this huge expenditure for the waste of military preparations can upset the economic apple cart. The economists, the learned men, the college professors, are all warning about this prospect. They are all saying, "We must expect that there is going to be a leveling off of the military expenditures. Then we must expect a recession, or a depression, or something of that sort."

What they really mean to say is, that if they don't keep spending 60 billion dollars a year—throwing it away, as far as any economic usefulness is concerned—and if they don't even increase it, and don't have a war, there is no way to avoid a depression.

Such a depression can be the precipitant of what we call a social crisis. Or, if they start the war in order to prevent the depression, among other reasons, then a social crisis will arise out of the war, in my opinion, in a comparatively short time.

This war in preparation is not the war against Spain of 1898, a mere adventure against a helpless foe. It is not the First World War, where America was not really engaged and enriched itself while the others fought, coming in only at the end of the war to tip the scales. It is not the Second World War, in which America again was immune from attack, and gained and profited out of the agony and slaughter and devastation of other countries.

No, this war is different. America will be directly involved on all the fronts of the world; and it will cost so many hundreds of billions of dollars that they won't be able to pay for it under the present budget, or double or triple the present budget. They won't be able to afford the living standards of the American workers as they are today, and they will be compelled to try to slash these living standards. That will be one element making for a social crisis.

And then there is the terrible, ominous, unprecedented prospect for America, the prospect of military defeats and the consequent anxieties of the mothers and the wives. Why, they have been two years in Korea, and they haven't been able to conquer it yet. And they have already got hundreds of thousands and even millions of American mothers and wives so agonized over their sons and husbands in Korea, that they turned the recent elections on the issue.

That's just one peninsula. The third world war they have in mind is to fight the entire world, on all fronts of the world. And do you think they can conquer the world in six months if they couldn't conquer Korea in two years? No, you must anticipate military defeats and consequent anxieties, anger, and protest, of which the reaction to the Korean war is a mere warning.

Out of all this, war or no war, and particularly if there is a war, the stable relationship of the classes in this country will be knocked to smithereens, and a crisis such as we have never seen or heard of will begin to unfold. This crisis which I anticipate, as do all Marxists, will be a drawn-out affair. In the course of its development, not necessarily all at once or in the beginning, but in the course of the development of the unavoidable social crisis coming in this country, two traditional features of bourgeois rule in the United States will crumble and fall. I refer to the American two-party system and the traditional American political democracy.

The real basis of both these features of American life and government has been the same. They are not simply the peculiar invention of American political genius. A peculiar American circumstance, rather, has made possible America's unique two-party system, which doesn't appear anywhere else in the world at present, and its traditional political democracy, which up until recent times was more extensive than anywhere else in the world.

The supports of this political system were the great riches of the United States, the social stability, the secure rule of the capitalist class, and the absence of any serious independent challenge by the working class. This is another way of saying that rich American capitalism ruled in its own house without any serious challenge, and could afford a comparatively democratic and benevolent rule in the political field. When these underpinnings begin to give way, as they must under the blows of a social crisis, then the superstructure, the two-party system and the traditional political democracy, will shake and then fall. Not right away, I repeat. That I do not predict. And not all at once. But they will fall.

What is this American two-party system, which so many people think is a matter of our will and our genius and can endure forever? In reality, it is not a two-party system. There are not really two separate class parties, as today in England. England has a two-party system, with the Tory Party representing the capitalist class, and the Labour Party based on the trade-union movement. The struggle between the Labour Party and the Tory Party is at bottom a political expression of the struggle for power in England.

What we have in this country are not two separate class parties, but two factions of the same ruling class—the Republican faction and the Democratic faction. This was a very good and convenient system for rich and stable American capitalism. From one point of view, it flexibly contained the antagonisms within the capitalist ranks. It gave a political expression for the conflicts of interests between different factions and sections of the capitalist class itself. In another respect, the two-party system, expressing the interests of two factions of the ruling class, but pretending to represent all the people, was an excellent safety valve for popular discontent.

When people got fed up with the administration power, they could always find relief for their dissatisfaction. The traditional American slogan always was, "Turn the rascals out." The only alternative, however, was to put another set of rascals in. That never did much good, but it gave the people a little satisfaction without disturbing the bourgeois rule.

It was a good system for them, and many capitalists surreptitiously supported the campaign funds of both parties. That's a well-known fact; it's what they call "insurance." They have one preference and give ten thousand dollars for the campaign fund, and then they have a second preference and give five thousand dollars. So, whoever wins is obligated to them.

That's a form of the confidence game known as heads I win, tails you lose, and it has been working wonderfully for a long time. And it could keep on working forever as long as the social relations are stable, and the capitalist class is not challenged on the political field by the workers.

Another advantage of the two-party system was that it gave the appearance of real political democracy. And this, I believe, is one of the biggest political fakes ever perpetrated in history. Of course, there have been all kinds of fakes in the world, but this one probably had the most suckers falling for it, and believing in it. That was its great value to the ruling clique.

The people thought they had a free choice every four years as to who was going to be president to represent them. But this was more appearance than reality. The machinery of both parties is tightly controlled by financial interests. The nominations are rigged every time. And the people's choice boiled down to a choice of two candidates selected for them by political machines, which in their turn were nothing but political instruments of the big money.

This political shell game was possible in its purest form only as long as capitalism was strong and secure and ascending in a stable capitalist world, and when there was no labor challenge to the capitalist rule in the country. Those conditions are fading away. The two-party system, in fact, has already been seriously shaken, even though outwardly the last election showed Republican versus Democrat as though nothing had happened in a hundred years. In reality the crisis of the thirties already began to undermine the two-party system.

Labor began to organize by the millions, to awaken to politics and to participate in an organized manner in the elections. The result of this uprising of the workers, engendered by the crisis, was the Democratic-labor coalition of Roosevelt and Truman. The traditional system remained formally Republican and Democrat, but the great change was that the Democratic Party began to represent a form of coalition of a section of the capitalist class with the organized labor movement.

This Roosevelt-Truman-labor coalition is significant historically not for what it did, although something was done, but for the trend it signified. The significance was not the coalition itself, and not even the social gains which accrued to the workers in the course of the twenty years of the Roosevelt-Truman regime. The real significance was the fact of labor participation in politics in an organized manner, for the first time. Despite the distorted form this coalition of the Democrats and labor movement took, despite all the illusions and disappointments that it brought—and it certainly brought plenty—this entry of the unions into politics in a deliberate, organized manner, for the first time, was a tremendous step in a direction that cannot be reversed. Labor is in politics to stay. That's the conclusion we have to draw from the present development of the Democratic-labor coalition.

The old Gompers policy is dead. It is a great misrepresentation for people to say, "All we're doing in the labor movement is what Gompers advised us." Gompers' slogan was "No politics in the union." But in this new development, which began under Roosevelt, not only do the workers as individuals go to vote at the polls, but the unions as unions go into politics. Every union in the country that isn't half asleep or half dead has its political action committee and its political workers who are just as much a part of the machinery of the union as the business agents and the other officers.

Labor is in politics to stay. But labor is not going to stay in the Democratic Party. And for good reasons. The imperative demands which labor must raise under conditions of the impending social crisis, will not and cannot be satisfied in the Democratic Party as it is now constituted. Even under the most favorable conditions, the participation of the organized labor movement in politics as a faction of the Democratic Party has yielded very meager results. For the past six years the top legislative demands of the unions have been a fair employment practices law and the repeal of the Taft-Hartley law. They couldn't get either one out of their coalition with the Democratic Party.

When the real showdown begins, labor on its side will be obliged to present real demands. The most militant and reactionary section of the capitalists, on the other side, will be setting out to smash the unions. What good is this Democratic-labor coalition going to be to the workers in such a situation? Why, it's really ludicrous when you stop to think about it. The strongest opposition to the civil rights program, and the strongest support to anti-labor legislation in recent years, has come from labor's "partners" in the Democratic-labor coalition, the Dixiecrats in the Democratic Party. That will not change. The capitalists, who in the last analysis rule the Democratic Party, will never permit labor to "capture" it.

Under the pressure of the first big crisis the Democratic Party, as now constituted, will split, and the workers will have to find another road. I don't mean to say that in the course of the crisis the coalition in government may not be tried again. There will be ups and downs. This current attempt of the American bourgeoisie to rule directly in their own name through the biggest millionaires in the country—this reckless experiment will go down in ruins under the first impact of the crisis. They may very well turn again to a new version of the Roosevelt-Truman-labor coalition. But it won't work. And the reason it won't work is that it can't give the workers what they need.

In 1933, when Roosevelt set up the first coalition, he had a large margin in his favor. There had never been any social legislation worth mentioning, never any unemployment insurance, never any kind of social security. Under the impact of the crisis, when the monopolists were scared out of their wits, it was possible for him to toss a few billion dollars to the hungry workers and put them on relief; put them to work on WPA, boondoggling and so on; provide unemployment insurance and old age pensions; legalize labor's right to organize. All this made the appearance of a great concession to the working class, which it was from the starting point of starvation.

But in the coming period, the whole impulse and drive and necessity of the ruling class is going to be not to improve social conditions, not to raise wages and living standards, but to slash them. That's what the crisis will be about, and a coalition government won't be able to do anything about it.

Consequently a coalition for class collaboration in government will not work the next time. Not under conditions of social crisis, when on the one hand the workers' demands will be far more extensive and imperious, and when on the other hand they will be threatened with the destruction of their unions. Labor will be compelled to take the next step in political action—to break the coalition with the Democrats once and for all, and to form its own party.

That, in my opinion, is by far the most probable line of development: the breakup, after maybe another experiment or so, the final breakup of the Democratic-labor coalition, and the launching of an independent labor party by the workers. There is already a strong sentiment in the working class of this country for such a step. Ford Local 600, the biggest local union in the world, voted the other day, after the election, for a labor party. The United Electrical Workers and UAW conventions have always been ready to pass resolutions for a labor party, if they had had a free hand from the officials. The sentiment for a labor party is held down by the bureaucrats, who think they can do better by deals with the Democratic fakers and the Dixiecrats.

The bureaucrats could put over this policy as long as workers were fully employed and getting fairly good pay. But this policy can't stand up against the pressure of a real crisis. The insurgent masses will form their own party, just as they built the CIO, partly in struggle against the conservative bureaucracy and partly with the help of a section of it. You must remember that this trade-union bureaucracy is not a solid crystal, and is by no means invulnerable. Its power and strength are greatly exaggerated. It also, as Marx said of society, is an organism subject to change, and is constantly changing.

The trade union bureaucracy is primarily concerned with its own selfish interest, but it is under many pressures and always yields to the greater pressure. The greatest pressure of all is yet to come. An antiunion assault is absolutely in the cards; is already planned and blueprinted, I venture to say. It is being delayed only by a little memo clipped to the papers in the file. The memo reads: "Hold for later setting of date." Everything else is planned and prepared.

The bosses will set out to bust the unions and cut wages and living standards. The rank and file will demand a counterattack to protect the unions and the living standards of the workers. Under this pressure the bureaucracy will split asunder, as was the case in the thirties with the rise of the CIO. In those days a part of the bureaucracy, Green and Company, went around the country like organized strikebreakers trying to prevent the organization of the unorganized. Some of the more far-sighted labor skates, like Lewis and Hillman and the others, who saw the great power that was in the making in this great movement, aided its development and put themselves at the head of it. But they couldn't "control" it like the old unions, not by a long shot.

In my view, a labor party will be formed under conditions similar to those under which the CIO was organized. And the party formed under such conditions and by such means cannot be a conservative party any more than the CIO could be a conservative union of the old type. Such a party will be of necessity, from the very first start, a radical, semirevolutionary party, with the most militant workers and the conscious revolutionists pushing it to the left.

And in this situation of political awakening of the workers, when for the first time the American workers as a class begin to turn to politics on their own account—then the revolutionary Marxist party, which has foreseen the whole development, which has theorized it long before it began, will find its own native environment, its natural field of work. It will become, in this great expanding situation, what is said in the scriptures, the leaven that leaveneth the whole lump.

The revolutionary party represents the future of the workers' movement in the present. It begins with a theoretical program which foresees the whole line of social development, and assembles its preliminary cadres on that basis. This theoretical understanding and faith in the future deriving from it are the conditions for the existence and dogged perseverance of the revolutionary party in time of stagnation and reaction. But for its rapid expansion into a popular party of the masses, it requires a great surging class struggle. That will come with the next crisis which is already ripening.

The tumultuous developments of the class struggle, under conditions of a developing social crisis, will explode in all directions, in all phases. The various prospective developments on the political and economic fields can be put into separate compartments, and dealt with serially, only for convenience in a lecture. But in real life—this is not a fabricated prognosis, but a deduction from the history of the development of revolutionary crises everywhere in all past times—in real life, when the social crisis strikes, and especially when it develops and deepens, the developments will be simultaneous, interacting on each other in all fields. This is what history tells us.

Under Roosevelt and Truman, the labor leaders' support of the imperialist government has been absolute and unconditional—and given in advance for any kind of crime on the international field. What was that monstrous policy of all the labor fakers based on? It was based on the purely selfish calculation that they, and a section of the American workers, would share in the spoils of world conquest. For that, they were willing to betray the world and all the people in it. They thought America's foreign policy could be like England's foreign policy in the nineteenth century, and yield the same results. By their conquest and enslavement of colonies and subject peoples, England's capitalists became so rich that they could afford, out of the superprofits, to throw a few crumbs to the bureaucracy and aristocracy of labor, and by that they bought its support. It was the promise and prospect of such a sharing in the spoils that bought the American labor leaders' support of American foreign policy.

That is the theory in the minds of Reuther and all the rest of the labor leaders in this country, their real motivation for supporting the foreign policy of America up to now—leaving aside the bunkum about their pious concern to spread American "democracy" all over the world by guns and bombs. They hope to do the same thing in the future, but it will run up against this snag: there are not going to be any spoils. There are not going to be any victories. There are not going to be any conquered peoples to sweat and slave to make America rich enough to maintain a high standard of living for the workers and fatten up the labor fakers.

On the contrary, American imperialism will encounter opposition everywhere; it will fight losing battles against revolutionary peoples, as already shown in Korea. There will be terrible casualties and incalculable expenditures, and the whole damned foreign policy, instead of enriching America and giving some crumbs to the workers, will have to turn back against the workers, to squeeze them to the bone to get the money to pay for America's barren and hopeless adventures on foreign fields. And that will signify the complete and utter bankruptcy of the labor bureaucracy in the matter of foreign policy.

Instead of that, they'll have to turn attention to the fact that the real issue is at home, where the drive is on to break the unions and slash the living standards of the workers. This will bring great strikes of unprecedented militancy, and attempts to break them by force. In the attempts to break the strikes, the beleaguered capitalists, feeling the ground slipping from beneath their feet; stalemated at best in a war, not on two fronts like Hitler, but on every front in the whole world, including the front of the class struggle at home—the capitalists of America, finally brought to bay, with their very existence at stake, will set out to break the strikes of the American workers with a ferocity and a savagery unprecedented even for America, where the labor movement was born in the most violent strikes in the world.

Where are the present leaders of the labor movement going to be when this kind of fighting takes place? They're not warriors, but as they call themselves, "statesmen"—labor "statesmen." These overweight palookas can't fight anybody, except their own rank and file, and they can't do that without the help of the government and the employers. Their favorite arena is the collective bargaining table. But the bosses are going to kick over the bargaining table.

These labor "statesmen" will not be fit for leadership in the new situation, any more than the old AFL skates were fit for the leader-

ship of the insurgent movement of the workers in the mass production industries in the sit-down strikes of the thirties. There will
be no bargaining tables. No government boards to settle things ami-
cably, recognize the union and give the workers a few more cents.
That's not going to be the bosses' program at all. They don't want to
give a few more cents; they don't want to recognize unions. They
want to knock the hell out of the unions, so the workers will have
no means of defense against the cutting of wages and living standards. That's what is in the cards. No friendly compromises at the
bargaining tables, but only mass battles and mass tests of strength.

The workers, under such conditions, must and will turn to militancy and throw up leaders of a new mold, just as the workers in
the thirties threw up new trade-union leaders out of the ranks. And
it is in just such a situation, when class collaboration is out the win-
dow and the class struggle is on the agenda, that the supreme expression of the class struggle, the revolutionary Marxist party, will
get a hearing and become the mentor of the militant new staff of
leaders arising out of the shops and the factories.

That's the prospective change on the side of the working class—
a change toward a new militancy, a new leadership, and the revolutionary political party rising in influence and power by virtue of its
character and its program. And on the other side, the capitalists
must and will discard all temporizing measures, cast off the democratic facade which they can no longer afford, and turn to wholesale violence against the workers.

Fascist bands will be subsidized and armed and hurled against
the strikers, against the union halls and all other workers' gathering
places and institutions. The workers, for their part, will have no
choice, if they don't want to be defeated and enslaved, as the German workers were defeated and enslaved under Hitler—they will
have no choice but to organize their own defense guards, meet the
fascist bands on their own terms and carry the battle to them.

American capitalism is not in love with democracy. It's no principle of American capitalism that we must maintain all the democratic forms—free speech, free press, free rights to organize, and all

the rest. The only principle the American capitalists have is the exploitation of labor, the extraction of profits, and the enrichment of themselves at the expense of the workers. That's their principle. If they can do it in an easy and smooth and quiet and peaceful way under political democracy, OK. That's the cheapest way. But when that doesn't work any longer, our wonderful, democratic capitalists will turn, with the savage fury of the German and Italian capitalists, to the bloody violence of fascism. They will finance and equip a fascist movement and check it straight up to the labor movement: "What are you going to do about it? There are going to be no more debates with you, it's going to be fight."

It will be a fight to a finish, and it will be fought on all fronts, from election campaigns to strikes and fights with fascist gangsters in the streets. Under the powerful impulsion of the social crisis which American capitalism cannot avoid, and which is already ripening within its body, all these developments predicted here, and many more, will erupt spontaneously, simultaneously, in one general process which cannot be arrested by any device. The irrepressible conflict will lead inexorably to a showdown in the United States of America, which will bear the name: The Struggle for Power.

The alternatives in this struggle will be truly terrible: Either a workers' government to expropriate the capitalists, or a fascist government to enslave the workers. Those are the alternatives.

Now who will win? Upon the answer to that question, in my opinion, the fate of mankind will depend. Trotsky once referred to America as "the foundry where the fate of man will be forged." That fate is going to be forged in the social crisis and the coming showdown battle between the workers and fascist capitalists for mastery of this land.

Who will win, in this greatest battle of all time, and of all places? That side, I say, will win which deserves to win. That side will win which has the will to win, and the consciousness that no compromise is possible. Power is on the side of the workers. They are an absolute majority of the population. And their strategic social position in industry multiplies the importance of their numerical majority at least a hundred times. Power is on their side. All they need is will, the confidence, the consciousness, the leadership—and the party which believes in the revolutionary victory, and consciously and deliberately prepares for it in advance by theoretical study and serious organization.

Will the workers find these things when they need them in the showdown, when the struggle for power will be decided? That is the question. We think they will. We think the workers and colonial peoples, in revolution throughout the world, will powerfully influence the American workers by their example. When all the world is in revolution, the American workers will remember their own ancestry and take fire too.

We think the American workers, who have never been Quakers, will demonstrate unexampled energy, courage, and decision when it becomes clear that their own destiny is at stake. We think they will find the consciousness, and therewith the leadership, for victory in the struggle for power.

And we think, finally, that it is our duty even now, in advance, in the period of preparation for the coming times, to contribute to this consciousness and leadership. That's why we belong to the Socialist Workers Party. That's why we're building it up. That's why we're inviting you to join us in the great work of preparation for the great tomorrow.

America under the workers' rule

Last week we discussed the coming struggle for power which will decide the question: Who shall be master in the American house? Our analysis showed that the advantages in this coming struggle lie on the side of the workers, and that their victory can be expected. This victory of the workers in the showdown struggle with the capitalists and their fascist gangs will culminate, at a certain point, in the establishment of a workers' government to rule the country.

Right at this point our differences with the anarchists are brought out most sharply. We don't hear so much about anarchism now as we did in my early days in the movement. Anarchism was then taken more seriously as a revolutionary tendency, but it made a miserable showing under the actual tests of war and revolution. Anarchism, in essence, is nothing but opportunism turned inside out, but it sometimes appears to be its opposite; and impatient workers, recoiling violently against a pusillanimous and compromising leadership, are often attracted to the high-sounding verbal radicalism of anarchists and anarcho-syndicalists and mistake it for the real thing. It is possible, therefore, that in the course of coming developments in America, anarchism could experience a certain revival.

That could cause a great deal of confusion just when clarity of program will be supremely important.

The differences between Marxists and anarchists are very serious and caused many polemical disputes and splits in the past, ever since the days of Marx and Bakunin in the First International. There were many points at issue in this great historic controversy, but the central point was the question of the state. The anarchist theory was that capitalism and the state would be abolished at the same time, in one operation. For them the revolutionary victory was synonymous with the abolition of the state.

The Marxists said, No, you are running ahead of yourselves. Marxism also envisages a society in which there will be no classes and no state, but does not agree with the contention that the state can be abolished in one step at the moment of the workers' victory. A transition period will follow when the workers will need a state for their own historic class purposes. Marxism regards the state as the instrument of class rule. It is not the general, impartial representative of all the people, as it is represented to be and as, unfortunately, many people think it is. The state, in its essential features, is the instrument of one class for the suppression of another.

That's the character of the present state in this country. Marxism gives the same basic definition to the state that will be set up following the workers' victory. The workers' state—in the transition period between capitalism and socialism—will have the same characteristics, in some respects, as the one that exists today. It will be a class instrument, its chief purpose will be to suppress one class in the interests of another. So far, it's the same thing as the Eisenhower state, with this slight difference: The state we envisage after the victory of the workers will be a governmental instrument of coercion in the hands of the working-class majority to suppress any attempt of the capitalist minority to reestablish their system of exploitation. The workers' state will be like the present state only turned upside down and put to the service of a different class.

The main features and role of this new state in the transition period are not for us a subject of imaginative speculation. The nature of society in the transition period between capitalism and socialism, and the kind of state, of government, it would require, were clearly foreseen and elaborated theoretically by Marx and Engels a long time ago; and the theory was applied in practice in the Russian Revolution of 1917 by Lenin and Trotsky. We have both Marxist theory and serious experience to go by in stating confidently what the general characteristics of the new state will be and what its tasks will be.

In drawing up their conclusions from the experience of the Paris Commune of 1871, the first attempt of the workers to set up a state of their own, Marx and Engels stated their theoretical conclusions on the nature of the state in the transition period with absolute clarity. Between the capitalist society of the present and the communist society of the future—they said—there lies a transition period of the revolutionary transformation of the one into the other. During this period the corresponding political state can only be the rule of the workers, the dictatorship of the workers, as every state is, in essence, the dictatorship of one class over another.

That is precisely the way Lenin and Trotsky, who were orthodox disciples of Marx and Engels, understood the the question and proceeded resolutely to apply it in practice in the Russian Revolution of November 1917. The theory of Marx and Engels on the question of the state and revolution has been powerfully reinforced by the experience of the great Russian Revolution.

So we can sum up this point by saying with absolute certainty that the working class, victorious in the showdown struggle with the capitalists and their fascist gangs, will not disband all government forms. On the contrary, it will take hold of society and set up its own government, its own state, and use all the concentrated power of this state to suppress any attempt at counterrevolution by the capitalists. At the same time it will use the power of the new state to reorganize the economy and direct it into new channels and new forms.

Certain things have been demonstrated in the Russian Revolution which prior to that time were maintained, and could be maintained, only theoretically.

On the positive side of that great historical experience, we can put down first, the demonstration that it is possible—as previously asserted by Marxism, but unproved—for the working class not only to remove the capitalists from power, but to set up a governmental machine to serve their own purposes and to maintain their power. Today, if anyone says, "It can't be done," the answer is: "It has already been done, and done successfully even under the most unfavorable conditions."

If anyone says: "This idea of a workers' government sounds good but it wouldn't work. The 62 million workers in this country wouldn't be strong enough to supersede the capitalists in power and set up a government of their own; they wouldn't know how to run a government; they have never been to school in statesmanship; they didn't study civics in college"—if anyone says that, the answer is: Only four or five million workers—that's all the industrial proletariat amounted to in tsarist Russia—four or five million workers were sufficient, at the time of social crisis, to overthrow the whole edifice of tsarism and capitalism and set up a government of their own. Moreover, they were able to maintain their power, not only against all the capitalists and landlords of Russia, but against the entire capitalist world which blockaded them and tried to overthrow them by military force.

Our programmatic statement that the workers will set up a government of their own in this country can hardly be dismissed as a utopian speculation—not after the demonstration of the Russian Revolution. Our confident assertion has the verification of practical experience as well as the scientific theory of Marxism behind it.

The second fact on the positive side of the Russian experience is the colossal achievement in the field of production. Tsarist Russia was the most backward of the big capitalist countries. Capitalist large-scale industry was only feebly developed there; it was far behind that of America, England, France, and Germany. But even with such a poor foundation to build on, it was demonstrated that production can not only be kept going without capitalists and landlords, but can be increased and multiplied. In the brief space of thirty-five years since the Russian Revolution, the most backward land of great capitalism has become the second industrial power in the world. That is attributed, and can only be attributed, to the elimination of capitalist private ownership, the nationalization of industry, and construction of planned economy.

In these two achievements of the Russian Revolution we have the practical demonstration, first, that the workers can rule; and second, that nationalized industry and planned economy can increase the productivity of the people. That is the touchstone of all social systems. The social system which can raise the productivity of labor, so that more things are produced with less expenditure of labor power, is the more progressive system. It is bound to prevail and to displace any less productive social system.

The negative sides of the evolution of the Soviet Union since 1917 have been the product of specific Russian conditions. We have no reason whatever to minimize or ignore the deformations of the Soviet state under Stalinism, truly monstrous and revolting as they are. But we should try to understand the causes of these excrescences before jumping to the conclusion that a workers' state in America would necessarily suffer the same degeneration.

There are great differences between the Russia of 1917 and the America of the present day, and these differences will all work in favor of the American workers when they come to power. In Russia the greatest difficulties began after the revolution. The overthrown minority of capitalists and landlords didn't submit. They organized a counterrevolutionary struggle which developed into a civil war, before the new state had a chance to consolidate. While Lenin was reading those great history-making decrees in the first Soviet assembly after the Bolsheviks had taken power, the counterrevolutionists were already mobilizing their armies, with the money and military support of the outside capitalist world. For five years—from 1917 until 1922—the main efforts of the new workers' government in this backward country, further impoverished and ruined by the world war, had to be devoted to a military struggle to maintain the new regime.

The *immediate* result was not a development of the productive forces but a further disorganization and disruption. Everything had to be subordinated to the demands of the war for survival against a world of enemies. There was a scarcity of the barest essentials of life. Daily life became a scramble for an extra piece of bread. Out of this economic circumstance, a bureaucracy arose, took shape, and crystallized into a privileged caste—as is always the case when there is scarcity. This bureaucracy, after a long internal struggle, eventually gained the domination of the country.

That is the negative side of the Russian experience, based on the economic backwardness of the country and its isolation in a hostile capitalist world. The attempt to march forward progressively and harmoniously, from the proletarian revolution to a socialist society, in a backward country surrounded and isolated in a hostile capitalist world, proved to be a rather difficult undertaking. It culminated, for an historical period, in the deformation of the workers' state into a bureaucratic police state.

But even under these adverse circumstances—and this is the point to remember—the new system of nationalized industry and planned economy could not be destroyed. Over a period of thirty-five years the new system of economy—the greatest achievement of the revolution—has proved its viability and its capacity to develop and expand the productive forces at a rate and on a scale never equaled by capitalism even in its heyday. That is the touchstone.

Things will go differently in this country, and there will be both difficulties and advantages in the difference. The difficulties will come first. The capitalist class in this country is stronger than it was in Russia; it has more resources: and it will fight with the desperate fury of an outlived class in its last stronghold. But once the power has been taken by the workers in this country, everything will be changed in their favor. And for the same reason.

Where Russia was poor and industrially backward, America is rich and highly developed. Capitalism has done its historic work in this country, and for that we should be duly appreciative. You see, we're not anticapitalist 100 percent; we're procapitalist as against feudalism, and chattel slavery, and industrial backwardness in general. We are procapitalist in recognizing the progressive historic role capitalism played in developing the forces of production, as illustrated to the highest degree in this country.

But in making this acknowledgement, we add a postscript: Capitalism has exhausted its progressive role; now it must leave the stage to a higher system. Capitalism has done its work here, so that when the workers come to power they will fall heir not to a ruined, backward, hungry country, but to the richest country with the most highly developed productive plant in the whole world. That's what the new government of the workers in America will have to start with.

What will be the form of the new workers' government? I wouldn't undertake to say positively, any more than I would undertake to say positively just how the transfer of the governmental power from the capitalists to the workers will take place. The two questions are connected, to a certain extent. Many variants are possible, depending on the strength of each side at the time of the showdown, and the disposition of the capitalists in particular.

If somebody says: "I would prefer to see the change effected by the workers' getting the majority in a fair election and taking power peacefully"—well, I wouldn't say I'm opposed to that. I would say, if it can be done, if the democratic forms are maintained and it can be done peacefully, that would probably be the most economical way of transforming the government.

Of course, even in such a case, you would have to do a very serious job of fixing up the constitution to make it fit the new needs. But that could all be done, provided the capitalists, contrary to the disposition of all ruling classes in the past, will agree peacefully to submit to the will of the majority.

But if history tells us anything, it is doubtful, to say the least, that they would agree to that. As the workers approach a position of political strength, where their majority in a fair election becomes a threatening prospect, it is possible, and even probable, that the capitalists will disregard democratic processes, organize fascist gangs and try to settle the question with armed force. The workers then will be obliged to set up their own defense battalions. In such circumstances it is quite possible, due to the stupidity, arrogance, unfairness, and historic blindness of the capitalists, that there will be some scuffling before the government is changed.

But it will be changed just the same, and however it may be changed, the new government will probably approximate the occupational or workers' council form; or will eventually be remodeled along that line. The present form of representation in the government by territorial units will probably be replaced by representation of occupational units. The delegates in the Congress will directly represent the workers in the shops, the factories, the farms and so on; not to omit the military units, which will also have a hand in the new regime as long as they continue to exist.

The workers' council form of government will be preferred because it is more representative and more democratic than the present form of American government. The new government will be primarily concerned with the problems of economy. The workers will have a means of exerting direct pressure and influence through their own delegates in the occupational councils all the way up from the local to the regional and to the federal assemblies.

The council form is more representative than the present form of government. For example, I don't think there are many sitting in this room who ever saw the congressman from their district, or even know his name. But there are very few of you who don't know the name of your shop steward in the factory where you work, and the delegates in the central bodies of your unions. They have something to do with your daily work and welfare and you have to see them almost every day. They are not something remote, like the government in Washington, but directly connected with the workers whom they represent. You can visualize the council form of government as just that sort of thing on an expanded scale.

The workers in factories elect their delegates to a local council, the local units combine in a regional body; the regional councils elect their delegates to the federal body. Control comes directly back, not to an election that takes place every two or four years, but to a shop council whose members can meet every day if they want to, right on the ground, and let their representative know what they want. Certainly the council form of government is more representative, more flexible and more democratic than the present form of government could ever be imagined to be. That's why I think it is reasonable to assume that the workers' government in this country will take this form.

What will be the first tasks of this new workers' government? Again, this is not speculative; it is not a mystery. The Marxists face this problem with an answer which was first theoretically outlined by our great masters; which has been demonstrated already in practice; and is now incorporated into the program of every revolutionary party in the world. The first task of the new government, once it has established its authority and its power, will be to abolish private property in the means of production. This will be done by one law, or by one decree, declaring that the banking system and all the key industries—all the big factories, mines, and factory farms; all the means of communication and transportation, public utilities, etc.—are henceforth public property.

I don't mean every little shop, corner store, and small farm. I mean the great industries which have already been organized on a colossal scale. They will be maintained and operated just as they are, with one small difference. Instead of a clique of nonproducers directing them for private profit, as at present, they will be nationalized and made the property of the workers' government, to be operated for public use and need, and not for anybody's personal profit.

Will these industries be acquired by compensation to the present owners, or by confiscation? This question used to be debated very heatedly in the socialist movement in the old days, but it is not really a question of principle; not in this country, at any rate. We say today: "It all depends." It is not necessarily more radical to say: "We won't give them a cent, we'll just confiscate." It is not necessarily wiser to say: "It would be better to compensate." I take a position in the middle and say, that whether the capitalists receive any compensation for the industries they claim to own—but which in reality they stole from the people—whether they get compensation or an order of expropriation without compensation—will depend on how they behave themselves.

If they want to submit to the majority and be reasonable, I think the government could easily agree to give them a certain compensation to avoid further trouble. America is rich enough. The workers' government could afford to hand out a few million, even a few billion, in order to prevent the development of a civil war. The government could do that, and might do it. It depends on the capitalists.

If they get nasty and continue fighting against the sovereign will of the majority, then they won't get anything. I take it for granted that once the workers have been victorious in a revolution and have set up their own government, they aren't going to be fooling any more. Everything is going to be serious and decisions will have to be carried out.

The next day after the nationalization of industry, or maybe on the same day, the new workers' government will lay official hands on all the gold buried in the ground at Fort Knox, and use this gold as the basis for American money. This will be the ironic paradox of history: that it took the workers' government to establish a sound dollar in the United States, based on gold reserves, of which, thank God, we have plenty in Fort Knox and other depositories. We can also thank the present rulers for accumulating them for us. Eventually, money will be dispensed with altogether. The fully developed socialist society will have no use for it. But in the meantime, the workers' government will have a sound dollar regulating the national economy, and no inflation.

Industry will be nationalized and operated according to a plan. Will that apply to all kinds of private property, to small farms, to small businesses, little stores? We don't think so. We don't think the new government would have any interest whatever in expropriating all the little corners of American industry and production. It would be wiser to let the small farmer keep his farm and continue to work on his own hook, and to let the little shops continue to operate.

The government will be busy with the great problem of nationalizing coal and steel and auto and rubber and all the rest of the big industries and the railroads. The small farms and businesses can fit into the new scheme and supplement it; fill in the crevices of the national economy. The new government would have every interest, not only in permitting it, but in encouraging it and helping out with credits, etc., until the small farmers and small businessmen decide of their own account that they can do better and live better by participating in the uniform national scheme and sharing in its benefits. It won't take them long.

But there are farmers and farmers. What about the factory farms such as those we have here in California—the great mass-production ranches, where hundreds and even thousands of agricultural workers are exploited in virtual slavery? They won't be left in the hands of parasitical bankers and absentee owners. They will be taken over by the state and developed as models of the new type of agriculture—the factory in the field.

The future belongs to this type of agriculture. In time, the historical anachronism of isolated, privately operated small farms will be preserved only here and there as relics of a backward age. Agriculture will be developed just as all other industry has developed, on the factory system with modern labor-saving machinery, with the scientific methods of soil culture, fertilizing, and so on. The aim will be to produce the greatest amount of food with the minimum of labor. The people, including the present farmers and agricultural workers, will get the benefit of it in the form of a higher standard of living, less hours of labor, and more leisure for living, for culture, and just to fool around and have a little fun.

The aim of the workers' government from the very start will be to increase production, eliminate waste, and improve the living standards of the people. And it will have to make good on this solid, practical ground. It will not be enough to say in government bulletins: "The new regime is morally superior to the old one. The new officials are more honest than the others." All this will be perfectly true, but, by itself, will not suffice. The new regime will stand or fall, like all social systems in history, by this basic criterion: Does it raise and improve the productivity of labor, or does it turn it backward? The new regime will have to "deliver the goods."

The American people will not be satisfied with official propaganda. They are from Missouri and they will say: "Show me." They will want better homes and furniture; more and better food and clothes; more tickets to good shows and circuses. Every citizen will want his own automobile and a good five-cent cigar; maybe also, for all I know, a better supply of fine wines and liquors. The new government will have to produce and deliver all that; that will be its first aim. And that's why it will nationalize industry, and reorganize production according to a unified economic plan.

Will this be superior to the present system? Will production be increased with less waste? That's for sure. After the Russian experience there can't be the slightest doubt about it. Today American industry operates blindly, without a general plan. The sole incentive for the operation of each and every factory in this country is the private profit of the owners. There's no general coordination. There's no concern about what's going on in other industries or in other parts of the same industry. There's no concern about whether the people need this or that, or don't need it. The sole driving motive for the operation of each and every individual corporation is the private profit of the owners.

The decisions on production are made, not by consumers, what the people need and want; not by the workers, what the workers would like to make; not by scientists and technicians who know best of all, perhaps. The main decisions on production under capitalism—what shall be produced, how, where, and when—are made by financial magnates remote from the factories, remote from the people, whose sole motive is profit in each case.

What are the results of this system, which Marxists call the anarchy of capitalist production? One result is wasteful competition.

Another result is the preservation of obsolete machinery and methods and the suppression of new patents. Twenty years ago the technocrats exposed the shocking fact that some of the most important patents for labor-saving methods and new processes are locked up in the safes of corporations. They bought the patents and suppressed them in order to prevent the development of more efficient methods by competitors which would render some present methods and products obsolete and reduce the profits they now make.

Consider the waste represented by the conspicuous consumption of the capitalist social parasites. That is absolute waste. The huge share of the product of American labor that goes to these nonproducers is all pure waste.

That's not all. Consider the waste of militarism and war. Just think of it! Sixty billion dollars a year wasted on the military budget at the present time, under the present system, which they say is the best in the world and the best that can ever be. Sixty billion dollars a year, wasted on military apparatus and preparation for war.

There is the waste of advertising, which is not only direct waste, but also irritation, which is another form of waste. You get so mad listening to the phony commercials that it makes you nervous, sets you to quarreling with your wife, and undermines your efficiency on the job. That's waste of human energy.

I would say, only 10 percent of advertising is useful—that 10 percent which comprises announcements, explanations of new processes and so on, which will be used under the new society. The other 90 percent of advertising is devoted to lying, ballyhoo, faking and conning the people, and trying to get them to favor one identical product over another, or to buy something they don't need and that won't do them any good, and then buy something else to overcome the effects. That is pure waste.

And then, there's another waste connected with advertising, as with so many other nonproductive occupations—the waste of human material, which really shouldn't be squandered. Just think of all the people prostituting their personalities in the advertising racket. Writers concoct slick copy, artists draw false illustrations, and radio announcers wheedle, deceive, and lie to promote crooked advertising campaigns. That is a waste of human personality, causing neuroses based upon the justified conviction of the individual that he is an absolutely useless person.

There are millions of such people, engaged in all kinds of useless, nonproductive occupations in this present society. Advertising is only one of them. Look at all the lawyers in this country. What are they good for? Look at all the landlords, lobbyists, salesmen, promoters, ward heelers, thieves, and swindlers—the million-headed horde of nonproductive people in all kinds of rackets, legitimate and illegitimate. What are they good for? What do they produce? All that is economic waste, inseparable from the present system.

Costliest of all the results of the anarchy of capitalist production is the waste of economic crises—the periodic shutting down of production because the market has been saturated and products cannot be sold at a profit. This is what they euphemistically call a "depression"—an unavoidable cyclical occurrence under capitalism.

I wonder what the future man, the really civilized man, will think when he reads in his history books that there was once a society, long ago, where the people might be hungry for the products of farms and factories. And the workers in the factory might be eager to produce and needing the work so that they could live. But because the hungry people couldn't buy the products, the workers weren't allowed to work and produce them, and the factories were shut down, and agricultural production was artificially restricted.

What will the people of the future think of a society where the workers lived in constant fear of unemployment? There is hardly one sitting in this room tonight, I venture to say—there is hardly a worker anywhere who knows for sure whether he will have a job six months from now or not. He can work all his mature life, forty or fifty years, and he's never free from that fear. His having a job depends, not on his willingness to work, nor on the need of the people for the products of his labor; it depends on whether the owners of the factories can find a market for the products and make a profit at a given time. If they can't, they shut down the factory, and that's all there is to it.

The workers' government will put a stop to this monstrous squandering of the people's energies and resources, which is the direct result of the anarchy of capitalist production. Just by cutting out all this colossal waste—to say nothing of a stepped-up rate of productivity which would soon follow—the socialist reorganization of the economy will bring about a startling improvement of the people's living standards.

The first condition will be to eliminate all private profits of nonproducers; to eliminate all conflicting interests of private owners of separate industries; to stop production for sale and profit and organize planned production for use.

When Marxists used to adumbrate the future along these lines, there was always some wise guy to say: "Ha! Blueprint! Utopia! It can't be done!" But that's precisely what was done in Russia, which had been the most backward of the capitalist countries. First they nationalized industry. Then they set up a central plan, and by means of planned economy they eliminated the wastes of capitalism and developed production faster than any other country in the world, until they became the second industrial power. And now the same thing is being done in China and in Eastern Europe. It is no longer a speculative prospect. What has already been done in other countries, can and will be done in our own country.

As one of its first acts, the new workers' government will appoint a central planning board to organize and regulate the entire economy of America according to one general comprehensive plan. What will be the composition of this planning board? Certainly no loudmouthed politicians, no bankers, no lawyers; I doubt whether there will be any preachers. But I would say, representatives of the unions, farm cooperatives, economists and statisticians, scientists, technicians, and consumers will be appointed as a matter of course.

What will be the aims of the plan? The central planning board will concern itself with the problem of the maximum utilization of all the resources and productive capacities in the country for one single purpose, according to one single criterion: what the people want and need.

The new workers' government, no doubt, will call in the atomic scientists and ask them to develop this new power for useful productive purposes. The prospect staggers the imagination. But from what has already been demonstrated in the field of destruction with the atomic bomb and the hydrogen bomb, we can easily recognize not only the possibility, but the probability that the atomic scientists will show the economic planning board how to take this new discovery and put it to work for the production of power for peaceful uses. It is easily conceivable that the whole problem of power will be revolutionized. We can visualize a great system of power stations generated by atomic energy, taking the burden of labor from the shoulders of half a million coal miners and transferring it to atomic-powered machines.

All science will be pooled and directed to a single aim: production for the benefit of all—in agriculture as well as in industry. There will be a revolution in the production of food when the economic side of it is lifted out of this terrible backwardness of private ownership and operation for profit and handed over to the direction of agricultural scientists, seed specialists, soil experts, and so on. They will go to work in earnest, unfettered by any private interest, and learn how to refertilize soil, and increase its yields. An army of chemists will be mobilized to attack all problems of economical and abundant food production. They will solve the problem of converting salt water into fresh water cheaply, and make the deserts bloom. One thing is absolutely certain, from what one can read of the scientific advances already made in this field and experiments in progress: The productivity of the farms, of the land, can be increased many times and there can be food in abundance for all.

There will be a great expansion of scientific and technical schools in this country where every talented youth will be entitled to go, free of charge, at the expense of the state. The opportunity to acquire a scientific or technical education will not be simply a privilege of one whose father is well-to-do, but will be the natural inheritance of any talented young person who wants to pursue a line of science to serve the people.

Vast sums will be set aside for medical education, research, and experiment. Not the grudging donations, here and there, from conscience-stricken philanthropists; not the present stingy appropriations from dollar-conscious legislatures. Just take all the money we spend on militarism and wars, and try to imagine what could be done if we spent only a small part of it on a program for health; a program to educate more doctors, and to make the doctors better; to enable them to live better and to get out of the money-making "business," which most doctors are in, and attend to the business of healing the sick alone. The workers' government, in its earliest period, will put a stop to this monstrous social crime of a shortage of doctors, while millions of ailing people go without proper medical attention.

The workers' government will open up new medical schools and research laboratories and put vast sums at their disposal. No shaking of tin cans and asking people to "give a dime" to fight infantile paralysis. The government will appropriate billions and send an army of eager and devoted scientists into battle against polio, cancer, heart disease, and other enemies of the human race. A comprehensive program for public health will come under the head, not only of humanity and of morality, but also of economy. When the people's health is taken care of better they will be more productive at work, and more goods of all kinds will roll out of the factories and farms.

We can say positively, on the basis of experience already accumulated under unfavorable conditions in the Soviet Union, that the early, the first, results of planned economy—eliminating all private profits and other waste, consciously employing more scientific methods, safeguarding the people's health—will be to double the present income of the workers, if they want to take it all. Or they may, and probably will, elect to take part of it to make a 50 percent improvement in their living standards and devote the other 50 percent to rebuilding and modernizing the factories and expanding the productive plant.

I'm not speaking now of the socialist society. I'm speaking of the first years, maybe of the first five-year plan of the workers' government. The first five-year plan will work such miracles in the field of production as to raise the problem of "superabundance," and what to do about it. The result of superabundance, or overproduction, as it is called, under the present system, is "depression": idle plants, and idle men; hunger; misery; homes broken up; children's education arrested; hopelessness for millions of people. The superabundant production resulting from the operation of planned economy, very likely in the period of the first five-year plan, will appear to the people as a blessing, rather than a threat. They certainly will not even think of shutting down the factories and throwing people out of work.

The "problem" can be dealt with in various ways. The first and most natural reaction of the workers will be formulated in a question: "If we're all doing well and living good, producing more than we really need in an eight-hour day—then why the hell should we work so long?" This question will arise in the councils of the workers in the shops at the bottom, and will be carried up through their delegates all the way to the top of the government.

And the logical answer will go along with the question: "Let's shorten the working day. Why should we work eight hours when we can produce all we need in four?" That may appear to be a simple answer to a complicated question. But many things will be simplified when the anarchy of capitalist production for profit is replaced by planned production for use.

That's only the beginning. You can count on a shorter work day, and there will still be abundance and superabundance. Then another question will logically arise in the minds of the enlightened citizens of free and prosperous Socialist America. They will not be narrow-minded, ignorant, and selfish isolationists, but will regard themselves as citizens of the world, concerned with all the affairs of the world and all its peoples, and will seek fraternal association with them on the basis of equality.

It goes without saying that they will grant immediate independence or statehood to the Puerto Rican people, whichever they prefer, and renounce all imperialist privileges and concessions extorted from other peoples by the deposed capitalist regime. They will go farther and say: "We've got human kinfolk in South America and Central America and in foreign lands, who haven't had the benefit of the great capitalist development of industry before they came to power. They're still working with inadequate machinery, tools, and implements. Why shouldn't we help them to rise to our standards, not only as a simple act of human solidarity, but also to put a firmer foundation under the world system of socialist cooperation?"

The American workers will so decide, freely and voluntarily. I can see them doing that out of the generosity of spirit and the world outlook which the vision of socialism has given to them. I can see them deciding, freely and voluntarily, to work, say, an extra hour or two a day, for a certain period, to produce agricultural machinery, fertilizers, automobiles, trucks, machines to make machines, and other things to speed up the industrialization of the undeveloped countries. And this will not be a loan or a piddling "Point Four"* with strings attached. They will simply say to their kinfolk in less-favored lands: "This is a little donation from the workers of the Socialist United States of America to help you catch up with us, and put a firmer foundation under the Socialist United States of the World."

"Missionaries" will be sent along with the machinery; not sky pilots this time, flanked by soldiers, but scientists and technicians accompanied by doctors. Such a gesture of solidarity, manifested practically in the voluntary labor of the workers for an extra hour or two a day, for a certain period, as a free donation to help industrialize Central and South America, Africa and Asia, will be one of the means whereby the workers in this country will take care of their "super-

---

* The "Point Four" program was established in 1950 to give technical assistance to underdeveloped areas. It was part of the Truman doctrine aimed at "containing Communism."

abundance" during the early period of the new workers' government.

The American way of life, which we hear a great deal about, will certainly begin to change under the workers' government. The people will not occupy themselves only with the economic side of things. The government will consider the welfare of the people in all other respects too. Again, I'm not talking of socialism. I'm talking of the first period of the workers' government in this country.

The government will enact a program of social legislation which will make the Roosevelt reforms appear as mere handouts in comparison. The new government will not offer a miserable pension to a worn-out work horse, if and when he reaches the age of sixty-five, if he has worked steady all his life up to then. It will not offer the worker a small dole against absolute starvation when his factory shuts down without asking him what he thinks about it. No, the workers' government will have nothing to do with such mockeries of social welfare. In workers' America—from the beginning of the workers' government, without waiting for the full development of socialism—no child, not one, will be born under a cloud of fear as to whether he is going to have enough to eat or not; or dependent upon whether his parents are in good health; or if they have some accident; or if the old man falls out of work.

By the law and the constitution the workers' government will guarantee economic security to every child from the moment of birth. The right to live securely; to have his health taken care of; to be removed from all fears of unemployment, of poverty, and of old age—will be automatically assured to every child by virtue of the fact that he was born in this country under a workers' government. Not only a right to live and to have food and clothes and a snug roof provided; but to have education. Education, as much as he wants, and as much as his talent calls for. Each and every person, without any exception.

That will be a very simple and natural and easy thing to do, because Socialist America will have the means, the abundance, the booming productivity—and all this will be produced for use, for the benefit of all. The system of planned economy under the workers' government will provide the people with abundance, and what is no less important, the time to enjoy it and get the full good out of it. I have spoken of the four-hour day, but that would be only the beginning, the first step, which is more than possible with the productive machinery as it is today. But the productivity of labor under the new, more efficient system will be expanded all the time.

And since there will be no need to pile up profits for the benefit of nonproducers; since there will be no need to find ways of wasting the surplus—the natural, logical, and inevitable conclusion will simply be to cut down the hours of labor progressively to the time actually needed to produce what is needed. The greatest boon, and the precondition for changing the American way of life into a truly humane, cultured, and civilized way of life, will accrue from the progressive shortening of the working day.

When the workers first began to fight for the ten-hour day in this country—I read in my histories of the American labor movement—the employers put on a tremendous campaign against it. They argued on moral grounds—"morality" of the capitalists is always happily married to their profit interests. They said: "If you cut down the hours of labor, if the worker doesn't work twelve hours a day, he will spend all his spare time getting drunk. The workers need to be working from dawn to dusk in order to keep sober and keep out of trouble." That's what they said. We won't hear such arguments in the future. When people get accustomed to leisure, they soon learn what to do with it.

The citizen of Socialist America will gradually move into a new state of affairs where his main preoccupation is no longer his struggle for individual existence—as it is today—but what he is going to do with that wonderful gift of leisure, the greatest gift, I think, of all. Leisure is the premise for all cultural development. Without leisure you have no rights. What's the use of being told you should do this, and you should do that, you should develop your mind and let your soul expand—when you're so preoccupied with work and trying to make a living and keep your family out of the poorhouse that you have no time for anything else? What you need is time! And for that you need an efficient system of planned economy to shorten the hours of necessary labor and give everyone the time and the leisure to think and reflect and loaf and invite his soul, as the poet said. A big start in this direction will be made already in the early period of the workers' government.

The regime of the workers' government in this country will be a democratic regime—democratic through and through. The abundance which the planned economy will provide for all, plus the time for leisure, for education and cultural development in general, will be the surest safeguards against a usurping bureaucracy, infringing on the rights and liberties of the people as in the case today in the Soviet Union.

When there is plenty for all, there is no material basis for a privileged bureaucracy and the danger, therefore, is largely eliminated. That will be the situation in rich and highly developed America under the workers' rule. From the very beginning, we will go in for real workers' democracy in this country; because, among other things, democracy is not only better for ourselves, for our minds, and for our souls, but is also better for production. Democracy will call out the creative energy of the masses. When all the workers participate eagerly in the decisions, and bring together their criticisms and proposals based upon their experience in the shops, higher production will result. Faults in the plans will be corrected right away by the experience of the workers; misfits and incompetents in the leading bodies will be recalled by the democratic process; officious "bosses" will be given the boot.

An educated and conscious working class will insist on democracy. And not the narrowly limited and largely fictitious democracy of voting every four years for some bigmouthed political faker picked for you by a political machine, but democracy in your work. That's where it really counts. Every day you will have something to say about the work you're doing, how it should be done and who should be in charge of it, and whether he's directing it properly or not. Democracy in all cultural activities. Democracy in all spheres of communal life—from A to Z.

I say, an educated American working class that has made a revolution will not tolerate bureaucratic tyrants of any kind. Another thing. The tradition of frontier democracy is deep in the blood of the American worker. He thinks he was born with certain inalienable rights and, by God, no brass hat, fascist gangster, or Stalinist bureaucrat is going to take them away from him. That sentiment will be another powerful point of resistance to any infringements on democracy.

The monstrosity of Stalinism arouses fears of the same thing in this country. These fears, in my opinion, are progressive, provided they don't lead to prostration before capitalism; because if you have capitalism you are going to have fascism, and that means a police state in its worst and most reactionary form. But that will not be a great danger, either—when the showdown comes. The American workers will take care of the fascists as well as the Stalinists. There will be no police state. There will be democracy, flowering as never before in the history of the world. But that does not mean that there will not be some repressions, if they are necessary. This workers' state, while it lasts, will still be a state; and the state is an instrument of force, used by one class to repress another. The workers' government must rule, and it is not going to promise anybody that it is something to fool with. Counterrevolution will not be tolerated. But outside that, the new workers' regime will be easy-going and tolerant, make itself scarce and keep its nose out of people's private affairs.

The scientists and technicians will easily be won over to enthusiastic participation in the great work of the new regime. For the first time they will be really free men, not only well rewarded in a material way, but respected and given their heads; not subjected to distrust and suspicion and not required to sign loyalty oaths; not regarded as second-rate citizens, mere hirelings at the command of some ignorant moneybag. The scientists will be honored as servants of the people, heroes whom the youth will strive to emulate. The scientists and technicians will come over with great enthusiasm to the new regime. There can be no doubt about it.

I don't think the new regime will have any serious trouble with religion. There may be some opposition from organized religion as an institution; the church bigwigs, especially the reactionary, fascist-minded Catholic hierarchy, will probably try to play a counterrevolutionary role in the actual struggle for power. But it won't do them any good. The workers will know where their real interest lies and act accordingly. People have a way of reconciling their religious convictions with their class interests. Besides, if they want texts, they can find plenty of sanction in the Bible for revolutionary action against money changers who profane the temple and exploiters who grind the faces of the poor.

Bill Haywood used to say: "No matter what the priest says about turning the other cheek, an Irish Catholic is a handy man on a picket line. When he's on strike fighting for his job and for his union, he finds a way of reconciling it with his religion." That's the way it will be in the revolution, and after. The communicants of the churches will find no difficulty in lining up with the mass of their fellow workers when it comes to a showdown fight for their own interests, for their own future.

And after the revolution, what interest will the workers' government have in suppressing religion, in persecuting people for their religious beliefs? None whatever, as far as I can see. Of course, the churches, as institutions, will be deprived of the support of the capitalist interests. They will have to get out of the real estate business and the charity racket; nobody will need charity. Each church, each religion will have to stand or fall on its appeal to its communicants. It will have to defend its dogmas against scientific criticism, which will also be free. But the new society will have no interest whatever in any kind of persecution of religious sentiments.

Counterrevolution can hardly be a serious threat to the workers' government in America. The workers are an overwhelming majority in this country, and their strength is multiplied by their strategic position in the centers of production everywhere. How is there going to be any kind of a counterrevolution against a government with such a broad and solid social base? I don't think the American capitalists will try it. The real exploiters are a very small minority. They couldn't get enough fools to do their fighting for them, and they are opposed in principle to doing their own fighting. The defeated capitalists will benefit from their own helplessness, and Trotsky thought it would not be necessary or wise to treat them harshly.

The little handful of recalcitrant capitalists who don't like what is happening will not have to stay and watch if they don't want to. The workers' government of rich America could easily afford to give them an island or two, for their exclusive habitation, and pension them off and get them out of the way. How big is Catalina Island here? That might be just the place for them. It will not be necessary to kill them off. Just send them to Catalina. Let them take their bonds and stock certificates with them—as mementos of bygone days—and give them enough caviar and champagne to finish out their useless lives, while the workers go on with their work of constructing a new and better social order. That's what Trotsky said.

War, and the threat of war, which made Soviet Russia's path so difficult, will be no problem for the American workers' government. Where would the danger come from? In Russia the danger of war was real and actual. But what country could attack the United States? If we are not the last capitalist nation to join the march toward socialism, our coming in will seal the doom of capitalism everywhere. The remnants of the whole world system will fall like a house of cards. The world victory of socialism will put an end to all national rivalries and antagonisms and, therewith, to all national wars.

The victorious American revolution will not stop very long with the forty-eight states. All the countries north and south of our borders will follow the United States in revolution, if they have not preceded it. In a matter of months, the new workers' government in the United States will join with Canada, with Central America, and with South America, in one great hemispheric federation—the Socialist United States of all the Americas. This new All-American Federation will work out a single economic plan for the entire hemisphere. This cooperative hemispheric plan will bring modern industrialization and scientific agriculture to all the countries south of the border, and raise up all the hungry people to full participation in a new and more abundant life in a better, more humane, and more plentiful society.

These tremendous developments—beginning with increased production and plenty of material goods for all, and then spreading into all fields of human concern and endeavor, will bring the people, by progressive steps, to the threshold of a new stage of society, without classes and without a state, and without any form of compulsion.

As the victorious people approach that new and higher stage of society, all the repressive features of the state will wither away and die out for lack of function. There will be no class to repress. All will be free and equal. The state itself will wither away. The government of men will be replaced by the administration of things. The transition period between capitalism and socialism will merge—without another revolution and without social convulsions of any kind, but simply by an inexorable process of development—into the socialist society.

That is the indicated line of social evolution in the United States, my friends—speeded up, as it will be, by a timely third American revolution. That is America's predestined road. We who see that, and strive to help it along, feel power and victory on our side, for we are in league with the future. In my opinion, to work for that future—with the sure knowledge that social evolution is working with us—is the most important, the most inspiring and the most satisfying occupation of all. The goal we strive for is worthy of anything we do for it or pay for serving it.

What socialist America
will look like

We Marxists conceive of socialism, not as an arbitrary scheme of society to be constructed from a preconceived plan, but as the next stage of social evolution. The preceding lectures dealt with the struggle for socialism, which develops in succeeding stages foreseen, understood, and consciously organized by the revolutionary party on the basis of a program. The subject of this lecture—"What Socialist America Will Look Like"—carries us beyond our formal program.

Our discussion tonight deals with the socialist society itself, which will grow out of the new conditions when the class struggle will have been carried to its conclusion—that is, to the abolition of classes and consequently of all class struggles. Our preview of the socialist society, therefore, is not a program for struggle, but a forecast of the lines of future development already indicated in the present.

The architects and builders of the socialist society of the future will be the socialist generations themselves. The great Marxists were quite sure of this and refrained from offering these future generations any instructions or blueprints. Their writings, however, do contain some marvelous flashes of insight which light up the whole magnificent perspective. The insights of these men of transcendent genius will be the guiding line of my exposition tonight.

Auguste Blanqui, the great French revolutionist, said: "Tomorrow does not belong to us." We ought to admit that, and recognize at the same time that it is better so. The people in the future society will be wiser than we are. We must assume that they will be superior to us in every way, and that they will know what to do far better than we can tell them. We can only anticipate and point out the general direction of development, and we should not try to do more. But that much we are duty bound to do; for the prospect of socialism—what the future socialist society will look like—is a question of fascinating interest and has a great importance in modern propaganda.

The new generation of youth who will come to our movement and dedicate their lives to it will not be willing to squander their young courage and idealism on little things and little aims. They will be governed by nothing less than the inspiration of a great ideal, the vision of a new world. We are quite justified, therefore, in tracing some of the broad outlines of probable future development; all the more so since the general direction, if not the details, can already be foreseen.

In attempting an approximate estimate of what life will be like under socialism, we run up against the inadequacy of present-day society as a measuring rod or basis of comparison with the future. One must project himself into a different world, where the main incentives and compulsions of present-day society will no longer be operative; where in time they will be completely forgotten, and have merely a puzzling interest to students of an outlived age.

Socialism will undoubtedly bring about a revolutionary transformation of human activity and association in all fields previously conditioned by the division of society into classes—in work, in education, in sports and amusements, in manners and morals, and in incentives and rewards.

But all these changes, which can be anticipated and predicted, will begin with and proceed from the revolutionary transformation of the system of production and the consequent augmentation and multiplication of the productivity of labor. This is the necessary material premise for a society of shared abundance. The revolutionary reorganization of the labor process—of the manner of working and of regulating, measuring, and compensating the labor time of the individual—will take place first and should be considered first, because it will clear the way for all the other changes.

Here at the start we lack an adequate standard of comparison. The necessary amount of productive labor time which will be required of each individual in the new society cannot be calculated on the basis of the present stage of industrial development. The advances in science and technology which can be anticipated, plus the elimination of waste caused by competition, parasitism, etc., will render any such calculation obsolete. Our thought about the future must be fitted into the frame of the future.

Even at the present stage of economic development, if everybody worked and there was no waste, a universal four-hour day would undoubtedly be enough to provide abundance for all in the advanced countries. And once the whole thought and energy of society is concentrated on the problem of increasing productivity, it is easily conceivable that a new scientific-technological-industrial revolution would soon render a compulsory productive working day of four hours, throughout the normal lifetime of an individual, so absurdly unnecessary that it would be recognized as an impossibility.

All concepts of the amount of necessary labor required from each individual, based on present conditions and practices, must be abandoned in any serious attempt to approach a realistic estimate of future prospects and possibilities in this basic field. The labor necessary to produce food, clothing, shelter, and all the conveniences and refinements of material life in the new society will be cooperative, social labor—with an ever-increasing emphasis on labor-saving and automatic, labor-eliminating machinery, inventions and scientific discoveries, designed to increase the rate of productivity.

This labor will be highly organized and therefore disciplined in the interests of efficiency in production. There can be no anarchy in the cooperative labor process; but only freedom *from* labor, to an ever-increasing extent as science and technology advance productivity and automatically reduce the amount of labor time required from the individual.

The progressive reduction of this labor time required of each individual will, in my opinion, soon render it impractical to compute this labor time on a daily, weekly, or even yearly basis. It is reasonable to assume—this is my opinion, but only my opinion, and not a program—that the amount of labor time required of the individual by society during his whole life expectancy, will be approximately computed, and that he will be allowed to elect when to make this contribution. I incline strongly to the idea that the great majority will elect to get their required labor time over with in their early youth, working a full day for a year or two. Thereafter, they would be free for the rest of their lives to devote themselves, with freedom in their labor, to any scientific pursuit, to any creative work or play or study which might interest them. The necessary productive labor they have contributed in a few years of their youth will pay for their entire lifetime maintenance, on the same principle that the workers today pay for their own paltry "social security" in advance.

On the road to that, or some similar arrangement, beginning already in the transition period which we discussed last week, there will be an evolutionary change of labor regulations, calculations, and payments. Emerging from capitalism, the transitional society will carry over some of the capitalist methods of accounting, incentives, and rewards. People first will work for wages. They will be paid in money, backed by the gold in Fort Knox, for the amount of work performed. But after a certain period, when there is abundance and even superabundance, the absurdity of strict wage regulation will become apparent. Then the gold will be taken out of Fort Knox and put to some more useful purpose, if such can be found.

When people will have no further use for money, they will wonder what to do with all this gold, which has cost so much human labor and agony. Lenin had a theory that under socialism gold could be used, maybe, to make doorknobs for public lavatories, and things like that. But no Marxist authority would admit that in the socialist future men will dig in the earth for such a useless metal.

The accounting arrangements automatically registered by money wages based on gold will at a certain stage be replaced by labor certificates or coupons, like tickets to the theater. But even that, eventually, will pass away. Even that kind of accounting, which would take up useless labor and be absolutely purposeless, will be eliminated. There will be no money, and there will not even be any bookkeeping transactions or coupons to regulate how much one works and how much he gets. When labor has ceased to be a prime necessity of life and becomes life's mere means, people will work without any compulsion and take what they need. So said Marx.

Does that sound "visionary"? Here again, one must make an effort to lift himself out of the framework of the present society, and not consider this conception absurd or "impractical." The contrary would be absurd. For in the socialist society, when there is plenty and abundance for all, what will be the point in keeping account of each one's share, any more than in the distribution of food at a well-supplied family table? You don't keep books as to who eats how many pancakes for breakfast or how many pieces of bread for dinner. Nobody grabs when the table is laden. If you have a guest, you don't seize the first piece of meat for yourself; you pass the plate and ask him to help himself first.

When you visualize society as a "groaning board" on which there is plenty for all, what purpose would be served in keeping accounts of what each one gets to eat and to wear? There would be no need for compulsion or forcible allotment of material means. "Wages" will become a term of obsolete significance, which only students of ancient history will know about. "Speaking frankly"—said Trotsky—"I think it would be pretty dull witted to consider such a really modest perspective 'utopian.'"

The ethic of capitalism and its normal procedure, of course, are quite different. But don't ever, dear comrades, make the mistake of thinking that anything contrary to its rules and its ethics is utopian, or visionary, or absurd. No, what's absurd is to think that this madhouse is permanent and for all time. The ethic of capitalism is: "From each whatever you can get out of him—to each whatever he can grab." The socialist society of universal abundance will be regulated by a different standard. It will "inscribe on its banners"—said Marx—"from each according to his ability—to each according to his needs." I speak now of the higher phase of socialist society, which some Marxist authorities prefer to call communism.

In the present society people are haunted by insecurity. Their mental health is undermined by fear for their future and the future of their children. They are never free from fear that if something happens, if they have a sickness or an accident for which they are not responsible, the punishment will be visited upon their children; that their children will be deprived of an education and proper food and clothing.

Under such conditions this "human nature," which we hear so much about, is like a plant trying to flower in a dark cellar; it really doesn't get much chance to show its true nature, its boundless potentialities. In the socialist society of shared abundance, this nightmare will be lifted from the minds of the people. They will be secure and free from fear; and this will work a revolution in their attitude toward life and their enjoyment of it. Human nature will get a chance to show what it is really made of.

The present division of society into classes, under which the few have all the privileges and the many are condemned to poverty and insecurity, carries with it a number of artificial and unnatural divisions which deform the individual and prevent the all-around development of his personality and his harmonious association with his kind.

There is the division between men's work and women's work, to say nothing of men's rights and women's rights. There is the division of race prejudice between the Negroes and the whites, which is cruelly unjust to the former and degrading to the latter. There is the division between manual and intellectual labor, which produces half-men on each side. There is the division between the city and the country, which is harmful to the inhabitants of both.

These divisions are not ordained for all time, as some people may think. They are the artificial product of class society and will fall with it. And a great fall it will be.

The emancipation of women will begin in the very first days of the workers' government, and very probably will be fully completed before the socialist society emerges from the transition period. The first condition for the real emancipation of women is their economic emancipation. That must presuppose the scientific organization of housework, like all other work, so that women too can have time and leisure for cultural activity and the free choice of occupation. That will imperatively require the establishment of communal kitchens, housekeeping services, nurseries and kindergartens.

The average poor housewife in this country is made to think that she was born into this glorious world for the chief purpose of fighting dust and wrestling pots and pans. That's not true. Women are capable of participating in all avenues of activity, in all trades, in all sciences, in all arts. Enough have already broken through to demonstrate that.

One thing I'm absolutely sure is going to happen early in the period of the workers' government maybe during the first five-year plan. Under the slogan of more efficiency in production, reinforced by moral arguments which are powerful in the case—the rights of women to leisure and freedom for cultural and spiritual growth— there will be a tremendous popular movement of women to bust up this medieval institution of forty million separate kitchens and forty million different housewives cooking, cleaning, scrubbing, and fighting dust.

Thirty or forty million women every day of the year trudging to the market, each one loading her separate basket and lugging it home to cook thirty or forty million different meals for thirty or forty million different families. What a terrible waste of energy, waste of productivity, to say nothing of the cultural waste, to say nothing of the imposition upon the women victims. The enlightened socialist women will knock the hell out of this inefficient, unjust, and antiquated system. The mass emergence of the socialist women from the confining walls of their individual kitchens will be the greatest jail break in history—and the most beneficent. Women, liberated from the prison of the kitchen, will become the free companions of free men.

The drudgery of housework will be organized like any other division of labor, on an efficient communal basis, so that women can begin to have some leisure too. Cooking and house cleaning, like any other work, can be done much better, much quicker, in an organized, scientific manner. Proper air-conditioning and dust-catching "precipitrons"—which will be standard equipment for every home—will take care of most of the house cleaning automatically.

I cannot see why the average housewife, who isn't specially trained for it or specially adapted to it, should want to bother with it. I cannot see why cooking, house cleaning, and janitor work shouldn't be one of the national divisions of labor, for which various people take their turns in the process for a certain number of hours a day, a certain number of weeks in a year, however it may be allocated. Or if some people prefer to live communally, as many have found it advantageous, they'll do that, and simplify things still more.

By this forecast I do not mean to draw a picture of regimentation. Just the opposite, for any kind of regimentation such as that imposed by the present social order will be utterly repugnant to the free and independent citizens of the socialist future. They will live the way they want to live, and each individual—within the limits of his general obligation to society—will decide for himself. Better, in this case, say "herself"—for old-fashioned reactionaries who ignorantly think they know what "woman's place" is, will run up against the hard fact—for the first time since class society began—that women will have something to say about that, and what they will say will be plenty.

What kind of homes will the people have under socialism, what kind of home life? I don't know, and neither does anyone else. But they will have the material means and the freedom of choice to work out their own patterns. These two conditions, which are unknown to the great majority today, will open up limitless vistas for converting the "home" from a problem and a burden into a self-chosen way of life for the joy of living.

Homes will not be designed by real-estate promoters building for profit—which is what the great bulk of "home building" amounts to today. The people will have what they want. They can afford to have it any way they want it. If some of them want a house of their own in the country, and if they want to have their cooking and their house cleaning done on the present basis, nobody will stop them. But I imagine they will evoke public curiosity and quizzical glances. People will say: "They've got a perfect right to do that, but they don't have to."

Every man can have his little house as he has it now, and his little wife spending her whole time cooking and cleaning for him—providing he can find that kind of a wife. But he will not be able to buy such service, and he'll be rather stupid to ask for it. Most likely his enlightened sweetheart will tell him: "Wake up, Bud; we're living under socialism. You've been reading that ancient history again and you've a nostalgia for the past. You've got to break yourself of that habit. I'm studying medicine, and I have no time to be sweeping up dust. Call up the Community Housecleaning Service."

I must also break the news to the Southern crackers and their Northern cousins, and other members of the Jim Crow fraternity, that under socialism America will no longer be "a white man's country." It will belong to the colored people too. They will own as much of it as anyone else and share to the full, without let or hindrance, all its bountiful prosperity and abundance, all its freedoms, rights and privileges—without any exceptions whatever.

The socialist society based on human solidarity will have no use for such unscientific and degrading inhuman notions as the idea that one man is superior to another because, many thousands of years ago, the ancestors of the first lived in an environment that produced in the course of time a lighter skin color than was produced by the environment of the ancestors of the second.

The Jim Crow gangsters who strut around in self-satisfied ignorance as representatives of the "superior" race may have to learn their mistake the hard way, but they will learn—or "be learned"— just the same. The Negroes will play a great and decisive role in the revolution, in alliance with the trade unions and the revolutionary party; and in that grand alliance they will demonstrate and conquer their right to full equality.

The Negroes will very probably be among the best revolutionists. And why shouldn't they be? They have nothing to lose but their poverty and discrimination, and a whole world of prosperity, freedom, and equality to gain. You can bet your boots the Negroes will join the revolution to fight for that—once it becomes clear to them that it cannot be gained except by revolution. The Black battalions of the revolution will be a mighty power—and great will be their reward in the victory.

As in the emancipation of women, the emancipation of the Negroes will begin with the absolute and unconditional abolition of every form of economic discrimination and disadvantage, and proceed from that to full equality in all domains. Race prejudice will vanish with the ending of the social system that produced and nourished it. Then the human family will live together in peace and harmony, each of its sons and daughters free at last to make the full contribution of his or her talents to the benefit of all.

The present big and crowded, ugly, unhealthy cities—I was asked at a previous lecture—what will happen to them? They will be no more. Once the transition period has been passed through, once all the problems of abundance and plenty have been solved, the people will want also to live right in the larger sense—to provide for their cultural and esthetic aspirations. They will have a great hunger and thirst for beauty and harmony in all the surroundings of their lives. These monster cities we live in today are blights of modern society. They will certainly give way to planned cities interlinked to the countryside. Everybody will live with the natural advantages of the country and the cultural associations of the town. All the Marxist authorities were emphatic on this point. The crowded slums and the isolated, godforsaken farm houses will be demolished at about the same time.

A new science and new art will flower—the science and art of city planning. There is such a profession today, but the private ownership of industry and real estate deprives it of any real scope. Under socialism some of the best and most eager students in the universities will take up the study of city planning, not for the profitable juxtaposition of slums and factory smokestacks, but for the construction of cities fit to live in. Art in the new society will undoubtedly be more cooperative, more social. The city planners will organize landscapers, architects, sculptors, and mural painters to work as a team in the construction of new cities which will be a delight to live in and a joy to behold.

Communal centers of all kinds will arise to serve the people's interests and needs. Centers of art and centers of science. Jack London in the *Iron Heel*, speaking in the name of an inhabitant of the future socialist society, referred as a matter of course to the numerous "Wonder Cities" which had been given poetic names—"Ardis," "Asgard" and so on; wonder cities designed for beauty, for ease of living, for attractiveness to the eye and to the whole being.

Farming, of course, will be reorganized like industry on a large scale. The factory farm is already in existence to a large extent in the West. Tens of thousands of acres in single units are operated with modern machine methods and scientific utilization of the soil, for the private profit of absentee owners. These factory farms will not be broken up. They will be taken over and developed on a vaster scale. Eventually the whole of agricultural production will be conducted on the basis of factory farms. The agricultural workers will not live in cultural backwardness, in lonely, isolated farm houses. They will live in the town and work in the country, just as the factory worker will live in the country and work in the town.

The separation between manual and intellectual labor will be broken down. The division between specialized knowledge of single subjects and ignorance on the rest, which is a characteristic feature of capitalism, will be eliminated. The half-men, produced by these artificial divisions, who know only one thing and can do only one thing, will give way to the whole men who can do many things and know something about everything.

There will be a revolution in art. The class society, which splits the population into separate and antagonistic groups of the privileged and the deprived, splits the personality of the artist, too. A few selected people have the opportunity to study and practice art, remote from the life of the people. At the same time, not thousands, but millions of children have the spark of talent, or even of genius, snuffed out before it has a chance to become a flame. Children of the poor, who like to draw already in school, soon have to put all those ideas out of their minds. They can't afford to be drawing pictures. They have to learn some trade where they can make a living, and forget about their artistic aspirations.

In the new society everybody will be an artist of some sort or other, and every artist will be a worker. Education will be for intellectual pursuits and manual occupations simultaneously, from childhood to old age. Marx was of the emphatic opinion that children should engage in productive labor from the age of nine, not at the expense of their "education" but as an essential part of it. From an early age, children will learn to use tools and to make something useful to the people. The child will have the satisfaction of learning by doing, and the satisfaction of being useful and productive even when he's a child.

Then older people will begin to treat him more respectfully. They will regard him, also, from an early age, as a human being, as a citizen, as a producer who shouldn't be treated as a baby any longer. He will be reasoned with and talked to and treated as an equal, not beaten or scolded or shouted at, or pushed into a corner. Marx said: "Children must educate their parents." And in some respects they will do that, too, when they get a fair chance.

There will be such a revolution in the relations of children and parents as we can hardly conceive of in this monstrous class society of the present. Parents often think they have been endowed by some mysterious supernatural power with the right to abuse and mistreat children. Primitive man never had such rights, never dreamed of such things. It is only due to the degeneration which followed the introduction of private property that the mistreatment of children and the double mistreatment of women became the rule. Primitive man in his natural state never knew such things. And the future society will know them still less.

Every child who has a talent for music or drawing or sculpting or molding or writing—and there is no such thing as a child without some talent—can become an artist of one sort or another. One who has an instinct and feeling for words can become a writer. There will be poets who will glorify the great theme of human solidarity, and they will not be starved and ridiculed as they are in this ignorant society. The poets will be honored, perhaps above all, because they have more insight than any others.

All-sided cultural development under socialism will not be some special gift or opportunity for favored individuals, but the heritage of all. The socialist man will have the most priceless of all possessions. He will have time. He will have leisure. He will have time and the means to live, to play, to grow, to travel, to realize to the full the expression of his human personality. And that will not be the exception, but the rule. There will be a whole race of people enjoying and expressing all those things.

I have a theory—again a personal opinion and not a program—that there will be two kinds of labor under socialism. All, without exception, will participate in the organized productive process, the source of the people's maintenance and abundance. But that will take up only a small amount of time, as already indicated. Then, I visualize another form of purely voluntary labor, unorganized, anarchistic, practiced as a means of artistic self-expression, and freely given for the general good or as a service of friendship.

Handicrafts, once the basic form of production, were virtually wiped out by the development of capitalism because of their comparative inefficiency, and many of the old skills of the artisans have been lost. The cooperative machine process, which produced more things faster and easier, eliminated handicraft as a serious factor in the productive process, and this progressive historical development can never be reversed.

But under socialism, where machine industry will be developed to the highest degree, producing even more abundantly many times over than at the present stage of its development, I can foresee a revival, a new flowering of handicrafts on a new basis. If this is theoretically inadmissible as a form of labor in the socialist society, perhaps my speculative suggestion can be considered under the heading of art.

I spoke before of the artificial division between intellectual and manual labor, and the half-men this division produces. The whole man of the socialist future will not be content merely to know what he reads in books, or to write books, or to confine himself exclusively to any other purely intellectual occupation. He will be trained from childhood to use his hands productively and creatively, and he will have plenty of time to exercise his skills in any way he sees fit; to do what he wants to do, what he likes to do.

I should imagine that under such conditions man, the tool-using animal, will assert himself once again. There will be a resurgence of free-lance cabinetmakers, shoemakers, hand tailors, bookbinders, etc. These artisans of the future won't compete with machine industry—that would be anachronistically absurd—but will ply their crafts as a special form of recreation and artistic self-expression, and to make gifts for friends. If they want to do it that way, who is going to stop them?

In the present society very few get a chance to do the work they really want to do, and thereby they are deprived of life's most solid satisfaction. "Blessed is he who has found his work," said Carlyle. But how many are so blessed? Most people do what seems best to make a living. Those who are able to choose their work, and to persist in it at all costs, are very rare.

Taking the present society as it is, I personally have had the work

I wanted, that I thought the time required, the occupation I was made for—that of a professional revolutionist. But in a socialist society, where there will be no need and no room for social struggles or revolution, the likes of me would have to find another trade. I have thought that under such circumstances I would be a cabinet-maker, as my grandfather was, a man who took pride in his fine work with wood and tools. Another would be a bookbinder, another a shoemaker, another a tailor—there are a lot of fine old crafts which will challenge the ingenious and the tool-minded.

Under socialism people will not fear to love their neighbor lest they be taken advantage of, nor be ashamed of disinterested friendship, free from all self-interest and calculation. There will be powerful impulses to give things to each other, and the only possible way of giving will be by doing, by making. There will be no chance to "buy" a present for anybody—because nothing will be for sale; and besides, everybody will be free to take anything he needs from the superabundant general store of material things rolling from the assembly lines. Presents, to mean anything, will have to be *made,* outside the general process. I think they will be, and such gifts will be really treasured and displayed on special occasions.

I imagine that when a man goes to his wedding, he'll wear a coat of many colors, like Joseph in the Bible, handmade for him by a friend who is an expert tailor, who has made it for him as a service of love. On holidays, he'll wear a handmade shoe, molded to his own foot by a friend who is a craftsman, who takes pride in his perfect work. And when he, in turn, wants to present a gift to a friend, he will make it for him.

Your house, the house of the well-regulated family, will have as the things it is proudest of, certain things specially made for you by people who like you. This easy chair made to your own measure by your friend so-and-so. This hand-mortised hardwood bookcase made for you by a cabinetmaker, as a gift. And those pictures and decorations on the walls—they were not machine stamped at the factory, but hand painted especially for you by an artist friend. And your important and most treasured books, which came well-bound from the print shops of the socialist society, have been rebound in fancy leather, by an old-fashioned bookbinder, a real craftsman. He does this outside his general contribution to the cooperative labor process, as a form of creative self-expression and as an act of friendship. I think it will be a great joy and satisfaction to be an expert craftsman in the coming time.

Morality, which in class society is either a hypocritical cover for material self-interest, or an escapist withdrawal from the harsh realities of the class struggle, will be changed inside out. The advancement of individual special interests at the expense of others—the highest standard of capitalist society—is summed up in the slogan: "Getting Ahead"—which means, getting ahead of others. It is the root cause of lying, demagogy, and deception, which are the central features in every election campaign, in advertising, and in all mediums of information and communication. The people are bombarded with lies every day of their lives. Capitalist morality itself is a lie.

There can be no doubt whatever that the new society will have a different morality. It will be a social morality based on human solidarity, having no need of lies, deception, demagogy, and hypocrisy. Those who cannot conceive of any human relationship without the "getting ahead" philosophy of capitalism say socialism would not "work" because people would have no incentives. They really have a low opinion of the human race. Incentives will not be lacking. But they will be different.

For one thing public opinion, uncontaminated by phony propaganda, will be a powerful force, as it was in the unspoiled primitive societies before people knew anything about private property and special class interests. The desire to be approved by one's associates will be a powerful incentive. In the new society the most useful people will be acclaimed, not the most "successful" in the business of getting ahead of others; not the rich exploiters, the slick fakers, the lying politicians, and the generals famed for slaughter.

The youth will venerate heroes of a new type—the scientist, the artist, the poet; the inventor who discovers a means of shortening the labor time necessary in this or that occupation; the agricultural expert who discovers a new way of breeding seed and making bigger crops. The applause and approval of the people will be the highest incentive and the highest reward of the socialist man.

Scope for ambition will not be lacking either. The socialist people will be completely alive and animated by driving ambitions. But their ambitions will have a different motivation and a different direction. Struggle is the law of life, and so it will be under socialism. But under socialism the struggle of men against each other for personal gain will give way to the struggle for ideas; to competition and rivalry in serving and advancing the general good of all; and to their cooperative struggle to complete the conquest of nature.

The people will struggle cooperatively—and through the competition of alternate plans—to move mountains, to change the course of rivers, to control climate, and to get the full benefit of all its changes. They will organize huge migrations with the seasons. Why should only the birds have the right to move south when it gets cold in the north? The rich have already claimed this right. The people who own New York, for example, don't live there much of the time. They spend their summers in Bar Harbor, Maine, where it's cool and breezy, and their winters in Florida, on the sunny beach. Some of them travel to other countries with the changing seasons. They stop over in New York only in the spring and fall when the New York weather is better than that of Maine or Florida. That, it seems to me, is a very sensible way to live—if you can afford it.

Under socialism, everybody will be able to afford to live comfortably and to travel freely, without passports. Can you imagine people living in Chicago in the wintertime, when they might be in California on a six-months vacation? Nobody ever saw the sun in Chicago from Labor Day to the Fourth of July; but here—I am told—it shines every day in the year—even when it's raining.

Some people who have lived in a frost-bound place all their lives may continue for some years, even under the new society, just from tradition, habit, and ignorance. But once you get them to come to the Land of the Sundown Sea on a trial journey, and see what California is like on the twenty-third day of January, they will never be the same again. And the daring souls, the pioneers who will find this out, will write letters back and the word will pass, and the idea will grow up amongst the people in the frozen north: "Why shouldn't we, with all our abundance—we can afford it, we have plenty—why shouldn't we travel around and enjoy climate with the seasons—just like the birds."

The people will have ambition, under socialism, to explore the great universe and to unlock its secrets, and to extract from their knowledge new resources for the betterment of all the people. They will organize an all-out war against sickness and disease and there will be a flowering of the great science of medicine. They will look back with indignation, when they read in their history books that at one time people had to live in a society where there was a shortage of doctors, artificially maintained. I believe it can be said with certainty that among the heroes of the new society, whom the youth will venerate, will be the doctors of all kinds who will really be at the service of man in the struggle for the conquest of those diseases which lay him low. Man's health will be a major concern, and sickness and disease a disgrace, not to the victim, but to the society which permits it.

Having conquered nature, having solved the problems of material existence, having taken care of the problem of health, the socialist man will begin finally—as Trotsky forecast in his brilliant work *Literature and Revolution*—to study, to know, and to conquer himself. The study and mastery of the body and the mind will bring the socialist man to physical and mental harmony and perfection, to the realization in life of the old aspiring motto: "a sound mind in a sound body"—producing a new race, the first worthy of the name of man.

Under socialism there will be no more private property, except for personal use. Consequently there can be no more crimes against private property—which are 90 percent or more of all the crimes committed today—and no need of all this huge apparatus for the prevention, detection, prosecution, and punishment of crimes against property. No need of jails and prisons, policemen, judges, probation officers, lawyers, bondsmen, social workers, bureaucrats; no need for guards, bailiffs, wardens, prosecutors, stool pigeons, informers, and professional perjurers. No need for this whole mass of parasitical human rubbish which represents the present-day state and which devours so much of the substance of the people.

With the end of classes and their conflicting interests there will be no more "politics," because politics is essentially an expression of the class struggle; and no more parties, as they are now known, for parties are the political representatives of classes. That is not to say there won't be differences and heated debates. Groupings, we must assume, will arise in the course of these disputes. But they will not be based on separate class interests.

They will be "parties" based on differences of opinion as to what kind of an economic plan we should have; what great scheme of highways should be developed; what system of education; what type of architecture for the wonder cities. Differences on these, and numerous other questions of public interest and general concern, will give the competitive instincts of the people all kinds of room for free expression. Groupings will be formed and contend with each other for popular support without "politics" or parties in the old sense of class struggle and the conflict of material interests.

In the classless society of the future there will be no state. The Marxist formula that the state will wither away and die out has a profound ultimate meaning, for the state is the most concentrated expression of violence. Where there is violence, there is no freedom. The society of the free and equal will have no need and no room for violence and will not tolerate it in any form. This was the profound conception of the great Marxists.

I recall that when I was very young, I read Jack London's *Iron Heel* and got from there for the first time, in one single reference, a glimpse of the socialist future wherein violence will be unknown. In a footnote to the manuscript in this great book about the ruthless class war in capitalist society, ostensibly written by an editor in the socialist society, the author calls attention to an enigmatic expression in the story. One of the characters is described as having the build of a prizefighter, and the editor thought it was necessary to explain to the citizens of the socialist society what prizefighting meant. This footnote reads: "In that day it was the custom of men to compete for purses of money. They fought with their hands. When one was beaten into insensibility, or killed, the survivor took the money." That had to be explained in the socialist society because they wouldn't know it otherwise.

Trotsky, in his last testament, written in anticipation of death, said: "Life is beautiful. Let the future generations cleanse it of all evil, oppression and violence and enjoy it to the full." Just ponder those words—Trotsky was a writer who weighed every word. His last injunction to the people who would follow him was: "Cleanse life of all violence."

In a talk with Gorky, Lenin said the same thing in almost the same words: "Our ideal is not to use force against anyone."

It is difficult for us to comprehend such a possibility, living in a society where even the smallest children are taught that they have to fight and scramble to protect themselves in a hostile world. We can hardly visualize a world without violence. But that's what socialism means. That was the ultimate meaning of our far-seeing teachers when they said that the state will wither away and eventually die out. They meant that eventually all violence of people against each other will wither away and cease to be.

The people will turn their attention then to that most important problem of all—the problem of the free development of the human personality. Then human nature will begin to change, or rather, to assert its real self. People will recover some of the virtues of primitive society, which was based on solidarity and cooperation, and improve them and develop them to a higher degree.

Leisure is the condition for all cultural development. "The glory that was Greece," justly celebrated in song and story, was the first great confirmation of this law. Ancient Greece, borrowing from other civilizations, produced the first truly cultured class. In some important respects it touched the highest peaks our race has yet known; and in the Golden Age of Pericles it came to its fullest flower. Its attainments in literature, the drama, sculpture, architecture, philosophy; in the beginnings of science and in the graces and amenities of civilized intercourse—are the original pattern from which Western civilization stems.

But that glorious Greece had a fatal flaw. Its leisure—and therefore its culture—were limited to a very narrow stratum of privileged aristocrats. It lacked the technological basis for *universal* leisure and culture. The society of ancient Greece rested on a base of dehumanized slave labor. It was surrounded by a world of barbarism. It was constantly embroiled in wars and eventually went down in ruins, and nothing was left of it but what is scratched on stone and preserved on parchment. A few ruins of the marvelous sculpture and architecture still stand to give an intimation of what was known and done twenty-five hundred years ago.

Socialist society will stand immeasurably higher than that of ancient Greece, even in its Golden Age. Machines and science will be the slaves, and they will be far more productive, a thousand, ten thousand times more productive, than the human slaves of ancient Greece. Under socialism, all will share in the benefits of abundance, not merely a favored few at the top. All the people will have time and be secure for an ever higher development.

All will be artists. All will be workers and students, builders and creators. All will be free and equal. Human solidarity will encircle the globe and conquer it, and subordinate it to the uses of man.

That, my friends, is not an idle speculation. That is the realistic perspective of our great movement. We ourselves are not privileged to live in the socialist society of the future, which Jack London, in his far-reaching aspiration, called the Golden Future. It is our destiny, here and now, to live in the time of the decay and death agony of capitalism. It is our task to wade through the blood and filth of this outmoded, dying system. Our mission is to clear it away. That is our struggle, our law of life.

We cannot be citizens of the socialist future, except by anticipation. But it is precisely this anticipation, this vision of the future, that fits us for our role as soldiers of the revolution, soldiers of the liberation war of humanity. And that, I think, is the highest privilege today, the occupation most worthy of a civilized man. No matter whether we personally see the dawn of socialism or not, no matter what our personal fate may be, the cause for which we fight has social evolution on its side and is therefore invincible. It will conquer and bring all mankind a new day.

It is enough for us, I think, if we do our part to hasten on the day. That's what we're here for. That's all the incentive we need. And the confidence that we are right and that our cause will prevail, is all the reward we need. That's what the socialist poet, William Morris, had in mind, when he called us to

> Join in the only battle
> Wherein no man can fail,
> For whoso fadeth and dieth,
> Yet his deeds shall still prevail.

INDEX

Playa Girón / Bay of Pigs

Washington's First Military Defeat in the Americas

FIDEL CASTRO AND JOSÉ RAMÓN FERNÁNDEZ

In less than 72 hours of combat in April 1961, Cuba's revolutionary armed forces defeated an invasion by 1,500 mercenaries organized by Washington. In the process, the Cuban people set an example for workers, farmers, and youth throughout the world that with political consciousness, class solidarity, unflinching courage, and revolutionary leadership, it is possible to stand up to enormous might and seemingly insurmountable odds—and win. In English and Spanish, $20.00

Cuba and the Coming American Revolution

JACK BARNES

There will be a victorious revolution in the United States before there will be a victorious counterrevolution in Cuba. That political fact is at the center of this book. It is about the class struggle in the United States, where the revolutionary capacities of workers and farmers are today as utterly discounted by the ruling powers as were those of the Cuban toilers. And just as wrongly. It is about the example set by the people of Cuba that revolution is not only necessary—it can be made. In English, Spanish, and French, $13.00

Pathfinder Was Born
with the October Revolution

MARY-ALICE WATERS

Pathfinder Press traces an unbroken continuity to the pioneering forces who launched the world effort to defend and emulate the first socialist revolution—the October 1917 revolution in Russia. From the writings of Marx, Engels, Lenin and Trotsky, to the words of Malcolm X, Fidel Castro, and Che Guevara, to those of James P. Cannon and Farrell Dobbs, and leaders of the communist movement in the U.S. today, Pathfinder books aim to "advance the understanding, confidence, and combativity of working people." In English, Spanish, and French, $3.00

Also from Pathfinder

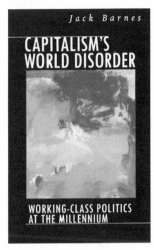

Capitalism's World Disorder
Working-Class Politics at the Millennium

JACK BARNES

The social devastation and financial panic, the coarsening of politics and politics of resentment, the cop brutality and acts of imperialist aggression accelerating around us—all are the product not of something gone wrong but of the lawful workings of capitalism. Yet the future can be changed by the united struggle and selfless action of workers and farmers conscious of their power to transform the world. $23.95

The Changing Face of U.S. Politics
Working-Class Politics and the Trade Unions

JACK BARNES

Building the kind of party the working class needs to prepare for coming class battles—battles through which they will revolutionize themselves, their unions, and all of society. It is a handbook for workers, farmers, and youth repelled by the social inequalities, economic instability, racism, women's oppression, cop violence, and wars endemic to capitalism . . . and who are determined to overturn that exploitative system and join in reconstructing the world on new, socialist foundations. $19.95

The Communist Manifesto
KARL MARX AND FREDERICK ENGELS

Founding document of the modern working-class movement, published in 1848. Explains why communism is derived not from preconceived principles but from facts and from proletarian movements springing from the actual class struggle. $3.95. Also available in Spanish.

Write for a catalog. See front of book for addresses.

Malcolm X Talks to Young People

"I for one will join in with anyone, I don't care what color you are, as long as you want to change this miserable condition that exists on this earth"—Malcolm X, December 1964.
Also includes his 1965 interview with the *Young Socialist* magazine. $10.95

Cosmetics, Fashions, and the Exploitation of Women

JOSEPH HANSEN, EVELYN REED, AND MARY-ALICE WATERS

How big business plays on women's second-class status and social insecurities to market cosmetics and rake in profits. The introduction by Waters explains how the entry of millions of women into the workforce during and after World War II irreversibly changed U.S. society and laid the basis for a renewed rise of struggles for women's emancipation. $14.95.

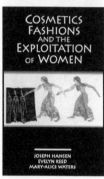

The History of the Russian Revolution

LEON TROTSKY

The social, economic, and political dynamics of the first socialist revolution as told by one of its central leaders. "The history of a revolution is for us first of all a history of the forcible entrance of the masses into the realm of rulership over their own destiny," Trotsky writes. Unabridged edition, 3 vols. in one. $35.95

Lenin's Final Fight

Speeches and Writings, 1922–23

V.I. LENIN

In the early 1920s Lenin waged a political battle in the leadership of the Communist Party of the USSR to maintain the course that had enabled the workers and peasants to overthrow the tsarist empire, carry out the first successful socialist revolution, and begin building a world communist movement. The issues posed in Lenin's political fight remain at the heart of world politics today. $19.95. Also available in Spanish.

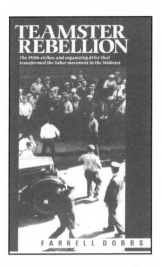

Teamster Rebellion

FARRELL DOBBS

The 1934 strikes that built the industrial union movement in Minneapolis and helped pave the way for the CIO, recounted by a central leader of that battle. The first in a four-volume series on the class-struggle leadership of the strikes and organizing drives that transformed the Teamsters union in much of the Midwest into a fighting social movement and pointed the road toward independent labor political action. $16.95

Socialism: Utopian and Scientific

FREDERICK ENGELS

Modern socialism is not a doctrine, Engels explains, but a working-class movement growing out of the establishment of large-scale capitalist industry and its social consequences. $4.00

Socialism on Trial

JAMES P. CANNON

The basic ideas of socialism, explained in testimony during the trial of 18 leaders of the Minneapolis Teamsters union and the Socialist Workers Party framed up and imprisoned under the notorious Smith "Gag" Act during World War II. $15.95. Also available in Spanish.

The Jewish Question

A Marxist Interpretation

ABRAM LEON

Traces the historical rationalizations of anti-Semitism to the fact that Jews—in the centuries preceding the domination of industrial capitalism—emerged as a "people-class" of merchants and moneylenders. Leon explains why the propertied rulers incite renewed Jew-hatred today. $17.95

U.S. Imperialism Has Lost the Cold War . . .

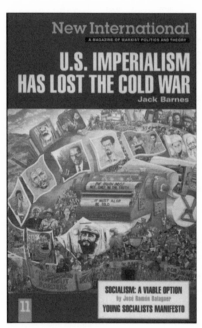

. . . That's what the Socialist Workers Party concluded a decade ago, in the wake of the collapse of regimes and parties across Eastern Europe and in the USSR that claimed to be Communist. Contrary to imperialism's hopes, the working class in those countries had not been crushed. It remains an intractable obstacle to reimposing and stabilizing capitalist relations, one that will have to be confronted by the exploiters in class battles—in a hot war.

Three issues of the Marxist magazine *New International* analyze the propertied rulers' failed expectations and chart a course for revolutionaries in response to the renewed rise of worker and farmer resistance to the economic and social instability, spreading wars, and rightist currents bred by the world market system. They explain why the historic odds in favor of the working class have increased, not diminished, at the opening of the 21st century.

New International
no. 11

U.S. Imperialism Has Lost the Cold War *by Jack Barnes* • Socialism: A Viable Option *by José Ramón Balaguer* • Young Socialists Manifesto $14.00

New International
no. 10

Imperialism's March toward Fascism and War *by Jack Barnes* • What the 1987 Stock Market Crash Foretold • Defending Cuba, Defending Cuba's Socialist Revolution *by Mary-Alice Waters* • The Curve of Capitalist Development *by Leon Trotsky* $14.00

New International
no. 7

Opening Guns of World War III: Washington's Assault on Iraq *by Jack Barnes* • 1945: When U.S. Troops Said "No!" *by Mary-Alice Waters* • Lessons from the Iran-Iraq War *by Samad Sharif* $12.00

Distributed by Pathfinder

These issues of **New International** are also available in the Spanish **Nueva Internacional**, the French **Nouvelle Internationale,** and the Swedish **Ny International**.

Revolution in Central America and the Caribbean

The Second Assassination of Maurice Bishop

by Steve Clark

The lead article in *New International* no. 6 reviews the accomplishments of the 1979–83 revolution in the Caribbean island of Grenada. Explains the roots of the 1983 coup that led to the murder of revolutionary leader Maurice Bishop, and to the destruction of the workers and farmers government by a Stalinist political faction within the governing New Jewel Movement.

Also in *New International* no. 6:
Washington's Domestic Contra Operation *by Larry Seigle* • Renewal or Death: Cuba's Rectification Process *two speeches by Fidel Castro* • Land, Labor, and the Canadian Revolution *by Michel Dugré* $15.00

Che Guevara, Cuba, and the Road to Socialism

Articles by Ernesto Che Guevara, Carlos Rafael Rodríguez, Carlos Tablada, Mary-Alice Waters, Steve Clark, Jack Barnes

Exchanges from the early 1960s and today on the political perspectives defended by Guevara as he helped lead working people to advance the transformation of economic and social relations in Cuba. In *New International* no. 8. $10.00

Distributed by Pathfinder